Breaking the Ice
My Journey to Olympic Hockey, the Ivy League, and Beyond

Angela Ruggiero

THE DRUMMOND PUBLISHING GROUP
362 North Bedford St.
East Bridgewater, MA 02333

First Edition
10 9 8 7 6 5 4 3 2 1

Printed in the UNITED STATES
ISBN 1-597-630098
LIBRARY OF CONGRESS CONTROL NUMBER: 2005929924

I would like to dedicate this book to my teammates. Hockey is a team sport where successes and failures are shared together. You are the people who have cried with me when we win, or lose. You are the friends that I have shared memories with and will continue to laugh with when our playing days are over. You are the reason I love hockey. Thank you.

Contents

Preface

When people think of hockey, they often think of fights, and when they think of hockey players, they often think of busted teeth and gap-toothed smiles—never mind that most players with busted teeth these days get high-quality replacements. In fact, I have been in one fight. But it wasn't in a women's league where I normally play. And I do have one busted tooth with a false replacement. But I didn't break it in a hockey game.

The fight happened in a summer men's league five years ago, when I was 20 years old. The game was pretty close at the time, and I went into our defensive zone to steal a puck from an opposing forward. The guy, who looked like he was in his mid-twenties, had it along the boards, so I went into the corner to pin him. I put my knee between his knees and pushed my knee into the boards, thereby stalling his movement. Then I used my stick to whisk the puck to one of the wings on our team. Nice play, no big deal. As I was skating away, the guy grabbed my jersey from behind and threw a hard punch to my face. Too bad for him, I was wearing a helmet with a full protective cage over the face. He connected but I hardly felt a thing. Out of pure instinct and adrenaline I threw a punch right back, then started swinging away with all my might. Because he wasn't wearing a cage, I pummeled his face over and over. I left my gloves on, so the punches wouldn't hurt me, and

I was getting the best of him. My teammates all circled around us cheering! I've often been the only female in a men's game, and in the past I was used to having my teammates defend me if any guy tried to rough me up on the ice, but I guess I was getting to the age and skill level where they thought I could defend myself. All I was thinking was, "I hope he doesn't rip my cage off!" We kept exchanging punches to the face until finally the ref came in to break it up. I was glad that was over and that my brother, who plays professional hockey, had jokingly shown me how to fight on the ice just the year before.

The broken tooth happened when I was shooting a promotional video for the credit card company Visa with the U.S. Women's National Team before the 1998 Olympics. The commercial setup was that we were supposed to run together through a set of double doors in the front of a facility at the U.S. Olympic Training Center in Lake Placid, N.Y. The idea was that we would burst onto the scene past the cameras. We were debating about who was going to hit the doors first, and a couple of my teammates nominated me because I was the biggest on the team, fast for my size, and, at 17, the youngest.

So they started rolling the cameras and I ran ahead of the team toward the doors. Trouble was, these doors swung in only one direction. I pushed from the wrong side, hit a door at full speed, and, crack!, busted one of my front teeth. My teammate Cammi Granato thought it was my earring hoop hitting the ground. I've got a great picture from that day with me in my gear, half my tooth knocked out, and my Team USA colors on. It's the quintessential hockey picture. And when I look at it, I smile, because I know it's all a joke and not what the picture seems to show.

Unlike the men's game, the women's game isn't built on bench-clearing fights and tooth-jarring body checks. In fact, women's ice hockey doesn't allow checking. I've heard a few jokesters say, "Oh, so it's not fun." You can decide for yourself, but I'll say this: when women's hockey first became an Olympic sport in 1998, a lot of people thought similarly. Following the gold medal game, at least a few minds had changed. Johnette Howard of *Sports Illustrated* wrote, "Sportswriters walked into the final grousing about having to cover it and walked out gushing that it was the best damn thing they'd ever seen. A felicitous line by *Washington Post* columnist Michael Wilbon, who called [A. J.] Mleczko 'the first leftwinger I've ever had a crush on,' was typical."

It takes finesse to work the puck away from a player against the boards without drawing a foul. And it takes speed and skill to close on an open puck, make a split-second decision, and pass or shoot. It may not be what the average fan first expects, but it makes for great competition and a great show.

In some ways, hockey's unexpectedness has been my life. I came to the game by accident and quickly fell in love with it. I had aspirations, but nothing grand. I never dreamed the game would take me around the world and even put me on top of it for a time. Nor did I have any idea that handfuls of girls from around the country would become like family to me and that the game's highs and lows would instruct me in many of the meaningful things I've learned about life.

Through these highs and lows, in different schools and parts of the United States, while living at different homes or while traveling abroad, I've had one constant: ice time. This is my story on the ice, but it's more than that. My growth in girls' hockey and then women's hockey follows the growth of the sport itself. I've learned so many significant things on the ice and through hockey. If I'm able to build the sport in any meaningful way by the time I've finished, then I'll have given back a bit of what I've taken from it.

CHAPTER 1

Going for Gold

From left to right, Sue Merz, A. J. Mleczko, Sara DeCosta, Alana Blahoski, Sarah Tueting, Jenny Potter, and me during the pre-Olympic tour before the 1998 Winter Olympics in Nagano, Japan.

That's Brandi Kerns on my left as we strike a Blues Brothers pose after we made the 1996 Junior National Team in Lake Placid.

At age 14, I shipped across country from my roots in the Los Angeles area to attend Choate Rosemary Hall, the expensive and prestigious Connecticut prep school, basically on a hockey scholarship. Much of what I remember most vividly from that year relates to my struggles to fit in. I was a Southern California girl amongst Yankee Brahmins, a fan of makeup, hoop earrings, body suits, and "that's rad!" expressions in the midst of subdued New Englanders who favored tattered corduroy pants, baggy college-emblazoned sweatshirts, and eyeliner-free faces. I also struggled to bring my grades up to par, but somehow I made it through and was gratified to succeed socially, athletically, and academically that tricky freshman year.

A couple of things that happened toward the end of that year made me realize I had a potentially much greater struggle, with potentially more public rewards, available to me. During the school year my dad had sent me a gift box of motivational items, one of which was a Wheaties cereal box with the Olympic rings on it. I pinned it to the wall of my dorm room to remind me of where I wanted to wind up. It became a silent companion piece to a hockey card that I kept deep inside my wallet, in a protective plastic case. It was the card of the U.S. men's 1980 Olympic ice hockey team, the team that beat the odds by upsetting the seemingly invincible Russian team. This improbable victory in Lake Placid launched the "Miracle Team" into the finals, where it won the gold medal. I was only two months old at the time of the game but I remember during my childhood seeing the highlights and hearing the sports broadcasters exclaim, "Do you believe in miracles!"

Another inspiration occurred during the Choate headmaster's commencement speech to the freshman class. In his opening remarks he mentioned my name, stating that I was a prospect for the 1998 U.S. women's ice hockey team, which would be among a handful of teams to play the sport during its inaugural year in the Olympics. His comment watered the seed of my ambitious goal. Students walked up to me afterward and said, "So you're going to be an Olympic athlete?" I shied away from answering, because the goal hadn't even seemed possible. Yet it had been put out there in public before a community of achievers that I was someone to watch. From that point on, students respected me as a student-athlete rather than as that colorful girl from California. Choate set the bar with the expectation that individuals could clear it.

That summer between my freshman and sophomore years, I tried out for and made the U.S. Women's Select Team, the core of which was expected to make up the pre-Olympic National Team and then the Olympic Team that would play in the 1998 Winter Olympics in Nagano, Japan. The Select, National, and Olympic teams are all organized by USA Hockey, the Colorado Springs-based national governing body for ice hockey in the United States.

Three years later, because I had already completed most of my graduation requirements, Choate administrators gave me permission to take off the fall and winter semesters during my senior year for the chance to become an Olympic athlete, just as they had publicly put out there three years earlier. At Choate, missing one day of class was enough to put you on a course to a failing grade. Luckily, I became an out-of-the-box student-athlete that the school supported. This allowed me to live and play with the U.S. Women's National Team on the pre-Olympic tour from August to December of 1997. If I didn't make the final cut on the Olympic team, I would be back earlier than expected to finish high school and graduate.

▼▼▼

As an impressionable 17-year-old, living and traveling with 24 other female athletes during the 1997 pre-Olympic tour had benefits other than sharing similar body aches and loving the game of ice hockey. It was a rock star tour with screaming fans and lots of travel but minus the substance abuse and late-night parties. Instead we had a curfew, nutritional requirements, and practice schedules. On the road with this group of amazing women, sometimes I couldn't help but let my youth show through. Then again, what did they expect from a player who still read *Seventeen* on the team bus while everyone else read *Cosmopolitan*? I was acting my age.

When I wasn't reading magazines, I was studying from a Scholastic Aptitude Test (SAT) prep book. The day that Assistant Coach Tom Mutch drove me into Boston to finally take the test, the team readied for a game in nearby Walpole. With my mind turned to mush from the intense concentration, I belatedly geared up and hit the ice. After a morning of blackening tiny ovals, however, I could barely hit a puck. "Ruggiero," coach Ben Smith said, "Ice is to hockey as (a) blue is to sky, (b) green is to grass. . ." Meaning, I think, that I needed to get my head together, out of the exam booklet, and be part of the team.

The women never gave me a hard time about being the youngest player on the team, yet I remember an instance when

I thought otherwise. Sue Merz, my future defensive partner and a stellar person, said to me one day as we left the ice, "Come on, kid."

"I'm not a kid!" This spewed out like an involuntary nerve twitch, before I had a chance to even think.

"Easy, kid," came the laconic reply.

Not until later did I realize that Sue called everyone "kid." As at Choate, my teammates respected talent, regardless of looks or age. All they needed to see from me was my consistent and solid effort when defending our territory on the ice.

▼▼▼

I was aware of our age differences and remained oversensitive to them. Small things that separated the girls from the women made me keep to myself in certain instances. For example, on one of my first trips with the team to Finland, I realized that these women showered naked in the locker room after games. This was new to me. Before, on the junior national team, after a game all the girls showered in their sports bras and underwear. I realized more women would notice if I simply did not shower and subsequently smelled the rest of the day than if I just blended in with the rest of the team after practice. It wasn't that I lacked physical maturity, because I didn't. It was just that the idea of being naked in front of a group made me uncomfortable.

While on this first trip, I waited to shower until after we returned to the cabins where we stayed. Later, after a game I tried to beat everyone else to the locker room. Then I could quickly undress, wrap myself in a towel, head to the showers, and finish before the others were even present. No lingering under the hot water for me—I could lather and rinse in less time than a NASCAR pit crew could change a set of tires. Eventually, during subsequent trips, I loosened up to the idea of showering naked in front of others.

Being around these high-caliber athletes for five solid months during the pre-Olympic tour, with so much downtime between games, made them more family than teammates. Essentially, I had two dozen older sisters who happened to be there to educate me on the next stage of my life—college. Given my young age, not surprisingly I started to emulate their routines on and off the ice. I realized that selfishness on the ice and cutthroat competition was not the brand of hockey that lent itself to the National Team. When you played, you did what was best for the team rather than the individual.

At this stage of my career, I idolized my defense-partner, Chris Bailey. I watched what she ate and starting replicating her post-practice routine of sit-ups, jogging, and stretching. To be a champion, I wanted to eat and train like one. At Choate there had always been a major discrepancy among skill levels on the team. Some girls were playing hockey mainly as an extracurricular activity, while a few of us were there with our eyes set on much larger prizes—not necessarily the Olympics but rather earning a spot on a college team. At Choate, I pushed the other girls to become better players, while on the U.S. Women's National Team my teammates pushed me.

The seriousness of the play inspired me while at the same time it slightly intimidated me. These women were slick and vocal. Often in the locker room, while we all dressed for a game, Cammi Granato or Alana Blahoski or one of the other leaders would speak up and help us gain the focus and direction to win.

I would try to emulate these players, along with Karyn Bye, A. J. Mleczko, Tricia Dunn, Katie King, Lisa Brown-Miller, Sandra Whyte, and Shelley Looney. These older players served as role models and offered me a new level of inspiration. Who needed the men's professional National Hockey League (NHL) when you could look to the stall next to you and emulate Granato, a player who had been on every one of the U.S. Women's National Teams to compete in the World Championships since they began in 1990?

After practicing and playing for hours at a time we needed to unwind. Between destinations I often worked on college applications, most of which asked for an essay about "something meaningful." Looking around at my unique current situation, I wrote about being the youngest player on the pre-Olympic tour. I penned these essays not knowing whether I would make the final Olympic team. At the end of the tour in December, after we had lived and played together nonstop for five months, the coaches would cut five players.

While on the road I narrowed down my college choices and received recruiting letters from such coaches as Harvard's Katey Stone, Brown's Digit Murphy, University of Minnesota's Laura Halldorson, Princeton's Jeff Kampersal, and Dartmouth's Judy Oberting. I waited to visit schools until the spring, but I stayed in contact with these coaches as well as talked with my team-mates, most of whom had already graduated from these and other universities. I realized that the Ivy League did not give scholarships, but rather financial aid packages based on need. I knew I qualified for "need" so my options remained open for all of my top college choices. I looked forward to being the second Ruggiero to go to college, behind my sister Pam.

I also realized that if I didn't make the Olympic team in a few weeks I still had plenty of options. This wouldn't be the start of my hockey retirement. Whatever happened, I still had to finish my senior year at Choate, make a few last memories with my friends there, and then decide on a collegiate hockey team and school.

In late December, just before Christmas, Coach Smith finalized the Olympic roster to twenty. I was among them. We were all given Team USA watches, which I just stared at while the other names were called. This being 1997, before everyone had a cell phone in their back pocket, team members stood in line by the pay phones to call their loved ones with the news. I couldn't possibly wait my turn. So I ran into town, jumped snow banks, and found a secluded pay phone where I could be myself as I dialed my parents' number. And when they answered the phone, all I could do was scream, "I MADE THE TEAM!"

▼▼▼

The next day I flew home for Christmas. When you see your family only twice a year, you become a guest in their home. By this time my family had moved from Southern California to Harrison Township, Michigan. The year before Dad had convinced the rest of the family finally that my brother Billy's hockey career was going nowhere fast if they didn't immerse him in a region chock-full of hockey opportunities. Going to stay in a house that harbors your family but no personal memories was rather odd. I had become a visitor, albeit a well-known one, to my family's house. After all these years, I realized family life was less about making memories inside an actual place than about making memories with loved ones, no matter where they lived.

When I arrived, the house was tidier than usual. Mom had stocked the cupboard with my favorite cereal, Golden Grahams. During the break I got to change my college essays to read that I had made the Olympic team. That, I thought, would place me in good standing in relation to other applicants. It wasn't every day you called yourself an Olympic athlete, but I was well on my way even if I hadn't won a medal yet. No matter who was young or old on the team, this would be a first for all of us. As one of more than eight hundred female athletes from around the world, I was ready to compete for a gold medal.

My mom, along with the parents of Shelley Looney and Lisa Brown-Miller, was conducting a fundraising campaign to garner enough money to fly over to Japan to see us play. Not living at home for the previous four years had left me somewhat uninformed about the inner workings of my family. When I voluntarily went away to boarding school and my family didn't have the vacation time or the money to fly crosscountry to see me play hockey or visit the campus, there was no guessing our relationship would change. You cannot see one another approximately six times over a four-year period of your youth and not expect the relationship to take on different dynamics. The people at Choate and my teammates had became a surrogate family. My shared memories with my blood family were paused when I left California for the east coast at 14. Essentially, a relationship cannot grow through a series of phone conversations. You can only recount what you've learned. Experiences are no longer shared. This doesn't mean we loved each other any less, though. Our relationships merely changed from adolescent to adult well before my eighteenth birthday.

Dad, who had been the guiding force leading me into hockey, silently let go as soon as I left for Choate and took the lead on my own. I no longer needed him to drive me to practice or arrange ice time in the wee hours of the morning. His role was over as far as being a hockey dad. I now had all the power to determine the role of hockey in my life. Most young people don't have this kind of freedom from their parents until later in life. I was barely in a bra when personal freedom landed in my own hands. Luckily, years later, I had enough discipline and drive that independence scored me a spot on a team destined for the Winter Olympics.

▼▼▼

The team spent the month of January 1998 in Colorado Springs, the site of America's other major winter Olympic training center. Skating at high elevations was the key to conditioning and preparing for our games in Nagano in February. For a month we lived at the DoubleTree Hotel and frequented Target and went to the movies during our off hours. Our coaches did not allow us to ski (downhill or cross-country), snowmobile, or take part in any winter activity that might lead to an injury. Our lives revolved around skating, shopping, and sleeping. This didn't seem like too much of a sacrifice considering the final goal, and in a way, it was a high school player's dream. To think all I had to worry about was hockey: no tests, no Saturday classes, no detention!

Finally, the team made the long flight to Japan one week before the Olympics' opening ceremony. We flew into Osaka, where as part of Olympic processing, athletes, coaches, and trainers were signed in and given their badges. We were then pointed in the direction of a warehouse and told to grab a shopping cart. I never expected the Olympics to be like an Oscar ceremony, complete with a grab bag of goodies. We pulled our carts up to each station within that warehouse and provided the vendors a size and color preference. They styled us with "Team USA" track suits, leather jackets, and gear for just about every occasion—interviews, opening ceremonies, closing ceremonies, daily wear, etc. They also gave us cell phones and free AT&T calling cards, which was great since my Dad and siblings couldn't be there.

They even measured our fingers for Olympic rings, which were a little smaller than Super Bowl rings but larger than most collegiate class rings. The ring said "1998 Olympian" on it with five small diamonds in the five-circle Olympic symbol. On one side of my ring it read "USA Olympics Nagano" and on the other side it read "Ruggiero" and "Hockey Player." If you won a gold medal, they changed the inscription to read "Gold Medallist." I figured in years to come that ring would look great in interviews in case I ever left hockey or needed proof that I actually did participate in the Olympics.

That night, Coach Smith tricked us. We had dinner and were exhausted, so when he said that we would have a meeting later that night at 8:30, we were all angry. At 8:30, we dutifully gathered, bleary-eyed, and wondered what could be so important. Coach Smith then said he just wanted to make sure we stayed up late enough to begin to adjust to jet lag, because we would have only a couple of days to do so. We groaned and headed for bed.

I quickly learned that national pride played a role in the Olympic Village. For example, teams drape flags over their apartment balconies. We put two flags up on the side. I was on the third floor with Jenny Schmidgall ("Schmiggy"), Murphy, Looney, and Sara DeCosta. When we opened the door our first morning in the village, Canada, which was right across from us, had roughly one hundred flags hanging off their balconies to show us up.

▼▼▼

Experiencing the Olympic opening ceremonies as an athlete was one of the highlights of my life. If you've watched it on TV, you know it's very formal. Behind the scenes, we were doing what you were doing—watching the ceremony, as other countries entered, only the whole U.S. Winter Olympics team was crammed into one big waiting room with a couple of TVs. The ceremony has the countries come out alphabetically, so the United States is near the end.

After a lot of watching and waiting, it was our turn. What was it like? Have you seen the camera view as players come out of the tunnel onto the field for the Super Bowl? Kind of like that. We stepped into a dark tunnel lit by dim lights. The United States Olympic Committee (USOC) wanted us to walk in lines, so we tried to get organized but in the dim light it was mild chaos and you could hardly tell what was going on.

We advanced through the tunnel, and near the end of the tunnel is a light (cliché, I know, but true). We came out of that tunnel, and the crowd erupted—I think that the cheer was larger than that given any other nation except Japan. Chills ran through my body, and that's when I fully realized, "This is the Olympics!" We circled the track, walking in lines and taking in the enormous crowds, the flickering camera bulbs, the music, and the athletes of the other countries.

Once we had circled the track, we were directed to our section in the stands, where we watched the elaborate ceremony as the rest of the athletes came onto the field. The Olympics had officially begun. This would be the pinnacle for most of the athletes. There were no winners or losers yet, just an international shared sense of belonging. We were all striving to be swifter, higher, and stronger. I felt part of history.

▼▼▼

During the next two weeks, whenever the team wasn't practicing or playing, we spent the majority of time in the Olympic Village. In the apartments, everything was a little smaller than in America. I remember the bobsled athletes often hit their heads on the doorframes. We also broke a few chairs in the room just from our size. Our feet hung over the edges of the beds at night.

One thing that the folks running the Nagano games didn't fall short on was the hospitality and food. No matter what country you came from, the giant cafeteria offered anything you wanted. Most of us stuck to the foods we knew, those that agreed with our systems. As an athlete before the biggest event in your life, the last thing you want to do is try some exotic new dish and end up doubled over in the bathroom. For me, bland food causes no surprises and fuels me when I need it most. The American athletes crowded around the pasta and chicken buffet, the cereal dispensers, and the salad bar. Had we wanted sushi or miso soup, we could have walked over to the opposite side of the cafeteria and ordered up. No food selection was overlooked.

In addition to the smorgasbord of food, the Village offered a campus of entertainment and necessities. I got a haircut, had a kimono made with my initials and Olympic rings embroidered on it, played video games next to Canadian figure skater Elvis Stojko and Czech hockey player Jaromir Jagr in the arcade, and checked my e-mail from fans around the world in the cyber cafe.

At another point, I had what I can only describe as a life-symmetry incident. Back when I was nine years old, because I was one of the few girl hockey players around, *Sports Illustrated for Kids* selected me, my brother Billy and my sister Pam, Brooke White (the daughter of a prominent local coach; she also eventually made the U.S. National Women's Team), future actress Alyssa Milano's younger brother Corey, and some other L.A.-area kids to appear with Wayne Gretzky in what was just the second issue of the magazine. Idolizing "the Great One," like I did, this was a highlight of my young life. So on this day I'm passing through the Village and there's Gretzky making an appearance. I approached him, introduced myself, and reminded him of that photo shoot nine years before. I asked him for another picture and he graciously accepted. He smiled and congratulated me on sticking with it and making it to the Olympics. I confess that at 18 years old, I still had similar giddy feelings seeing my childhood idol.

At another point, I ran into figure skater and soon-to-be Olympic gold medalist Tara Lipinski. At four-foot-ten and 86 pounds, she was the smallest athlete at the Olympics, while at five-foot-nine and 180 pounds, I was the biggest female athlete on the U.S. team. I pointed this out to her and she laughed. We took a picture together—the smallest and the largest at the Games.

As great as the place is, the Olympic Village has a cloistered feel. No one except employees and athletes can enter the complex—not even members of athletes' families. Athletes have to show their badge to enter.

That year we also had to pass a gender test, a rule that came about because of some men who had tried to compete as women in previous Olympic games. Officials would swab the inside of athletes' cheeks to see if they had the right amount of hormones. Eventually, because of political pressure, that practice was discarded, but at Nagano female athletes had to show a gender card, as well as an ID card, to enter the village. I was amused, however, at the fact that I had a badge to confirm that I was a woman.

Perhaps the coolest thing at the Village is that they show you each sport on television, but with no commercials. You can just watch the event without any commentary, and you can channel surf for any sport. When we weren't practicing or playing, we watched many U.S. athletes compete in different sports, and I learned a lot about people and sports I had never known before.

To practice, we had to bus many miles every day, with all our gear already on. The U.S. men's hockey team, made up mostly of professional players from the NHL, had to do the same thing that year, so there was no complaining. Each team had a specific time slot for a closed practice session—no media and no fans allowed. We didn't spy on the other teams' practices and they didn't spy on us.

▼▼▼

During my tenure as an Olympic defenseman, the coaches made my role simple: play stay-at-home defense. They didn't want me to take chances by rushing the puck up the ice, but rather to stay back and help to defend our goal in the event opposing players blew past our forwards. Thus, I would end up not registering a single point in my first Olympics because my role was to prevent the other team from scoring, plain and simple.

People often ask me what I remember of each game. Actually, I remember vividly two games: Canada and Canada. Even when I was interviewed immediately following the Olympics by a member of USA Hockey, those were the most memorable games, and little else stood out to me. *But it was the Olympics,* you might say.

The reason relates to the nature of women's ice hockey at that time. The sport, along with curling and snowboarding, was brand new to the Olympics that year. Only six nations competed in women's ice hockey at the Games: Sweden, Finland, China, Japan, Canada, and the United States. Of those teams, only three had ever won medals of any sort in international competition— Finland, the United States, and Canada—and of those, only the United States and Canadian teams had ever won gold medals.

At the Games, the tournament was set up as a round robin. In the first round, each team played every other team one time. The two teams with the best records then advanced to the gold medal game. The third- and fourth-place teams advanced to the bronze medal game, and the other two were eliminated.

We started the day after the opening ceremonies by shutting out China 5–0, and followed that with a 7–1 drubbing of Sweden. Two days later, Finland worked us hard before folding and we won 4–2. The next day, we pounded the hometown team, Japan, 10–0. That left only Canada to play. By that time, they had also coasted through the other four competitors, meaning that no matter what happened in the fifth game, both teams were going to be playing each other again in the gold medal game.

But that final round-robin game was the key to the whole tournament and is the first Olympic game that I have etched deeply into my memory. Why? In 1990, the International Ice Hockey Federation (IIHF) had held the first Women's World Championships. Canada defeated the United States, 5–2. Thereafter, Canada defeated the United States in every major international tournament until 1997. They were the team to beat in the world. Finally, in the 1997 Three Nations Cup in Lake Placid, we bested Canada and Finland over nine games to claim Team USA's first international tournament gold. Between 1997 and 1998, we played Canada 13 times, and coming into the Olympics, Canada owned a 7–6 edge against us.

But this rivalry was much more than just a longstanding battle between frequent opponents. Emotions and tensions ran high between the teams. In 1997, during the Three Nations tournament, we lost in an early round to Canada. Rather than leave us alone in our locker room, Coach Smith made us stand in the hallway and listen to the Canadians celebrate in their locker room. We decided then and there we had taken enough and ultimately we claimed the Cup.

Even though this last first-round game was supposed to be meaningless, we took the ice with fire in our veins. And it nearly wrecked us. Early in the first period, forward A. J. Mleczko knocked over a Canadian player right in front of the Canadian bench, drawing a penalty but also inflaming the Canadians. Like the rest of the American team, I was too fired up, playing without enough discipline and drawing two body-checking penalties. One of these was a major penalty that landed me 10 minutes in the penalty box (most penalties are for only two minutes). Midway through the second period, we were down 4–1, and all of the Canadians' goals had come while at least one of us was sitting in the penalty box.

Coach Smith called a timeout in the middle of that period. He gathered us around and spoke calmly. He told us we were pressing too hard, playing too emotionally, and also that we were thinking too much. We just needed to step back and let the game to us, to let it develop and then go with its flow.

Somehow, that worked. Halfway through the third period, our whole tournament changed. We scored a goal that made it 4–2. Between that goal and the end of the game, we punched in five more goals and won 7–4. It was the first time in history that Canada had ever given up six unanswered goals, and more important, it gave us a huge boost of confidence coming into the gold medal game.

▼▼▼

If the first-round game was erratic and full of emotion, the gold medal game might be the best, most complete, team-first game I've ever been a part of. Our confidence was brimming when we took the ice—we had beaten Canada three days before, and they still had to face our streak of six unanswered goals. Beyond that, there was a connection between all of us on the team. Most of us had been playing together for two years, and for many of the older women the gold medal game was a culmination. I would later understand that it meant more to those older players than it could yet mean for me, because of how they had given so much to the sport and to the U.S. team.

We also knew that it might be the last time many of us would play together. At the very least, following the Games, we would be going our separate ways back to school or jobs or families, and some of us might not come back to the national team.

We skated that day with a mixture of confidence and connectedness. That team feeling was crucial to two of our three goals, and perhaps my most important role that day was something you don't see on the scoreboard. Coach Smith decided that on power plays, Sandra Whyte would take the point instead of me. That is, when a penalty on the other team gave us a temporary advantage of playing with five skaters (not including the goalie) on the ice to the other team's four, she would be positioned at our blue line, making passes and shooting and basically directing the offensive action. I'll be honest—that gnawed at me a little bit. But Smith felt like she was just a bit faster than I was, and perhaps he might have also been relying on her veteran experience. I remember playing my regular shifts, but then yielding to Sandra on the power plays. And rather than be mad about it I consciously told myself that this was for the team, that I was willing to do whatever was necessary to make the team better, and if this is what Coach Smith felt made the team better, I would support it. Two of our goals came on assists from Sandra during power plays—each with her trademark quickness. Sandra also scored our third and final goal of the game, an empty-netter (desperate to tie the score, Canada took their goalie off the ice to add another offensive skater) with about ten seconds left in the game. I was so excited I actually knocked Sandra over when she put us up 3–1, then had to get control of myself for the final few seconds.

With one shift left before the buzzer sounded, Assistant Coach Mutch looked over at me and said, "Rugger, are you ready for this?" I had envisioned the final minutes of the gold medal game months and months before. Before games I often took a nap. There was a make-believe video that I had created and produced that played in my head. And in that short film, complete with a muted audio track for most of it, I sprinted down the ice and jumped on my teammates as the clock hit zero. My strength knocked down a few skaters and then the film's audio track turned on. Screams and a "dog pile" of players jumping on each other ensued. The gloves flew through the air and landed like rose petals displayed on a dinner table set for two.

In reality, this was exactly how it happened after the final buzzer sounded. What I didn't feel in my pregame film was the way my heart rate dropped and my legs felt light. Time seemed to stand still as the clock ticked down, slowly propelling me to a different plane of reality. My mind was no longer engaged in active strategizing as it was during competition, but turned inward to a billowy silence that eventually erupted when I collided with my clan on the ice. Then, it was as if the stadium would never be quiet again. A voice inside my brain whispered, "Don't forget this moment. Ever." That prompted me to leave the dog pile, sprint to the opposite end of the ice, pick up the game puck, stuff it down my pants, and sprint back to the dog pile. The puck was my memento of a life with women who I had grown to love and respect. (I later gave this puck to my dad, who now says that it's his most prized possession.)

Some time during the celebration, I was so overwhelmed by the joy of the moment that, while I was skating along the boards, I grabbed an American flag that someone was holding and dashed around the rink, waving it in the air. It was just the over-excitement of an 18-year-old who felt she had reached the top of the world. But apparently it was a good image—it got picked up by print and television media across the world and is something, to this day, that visually represents the team's joy in our victory, our country, and our sport.

For me, the victory was the purest I've ever experienced. Our team was perfectly unified in that final game. There were no Olympic veterans or previous Olympic stars, nor was there big money involved—we thought that much of the media would hardly pay attention. In a way, that moment of unity absolved the pattern of connect-and-disconnect I had had in my family from our years of separation. At least temporarily, here was another family atmosphere for me, one where anything was possible through our strength in each other.

▼▼▼

Later, watching the television broadcast of all of us lined up for the gold medal ceremony, I noticed how off-key we were while singing the national anthem. We were terrible singers—tone deaf, apparently. We had spontaneously grabbed hands in unison. Near the end I pumped my hand in the air as I held a bouquet of wildflowers and a small American flag. The gold medal, which weighs more than a pound and is about the size of a diner's coffee saucer, hung around my neck on a shiny blue ribbon. We had exceeded expectations by defeating the favored Canadians, the team that had dominated international competitions during the 1990s.

Our spontaneous, if inept, singing of the national anthem captured a lot of attention, and I realize now that the joy of the experience went broader and deeper than I knew at the time. Leigh Montville wrote for CNN and *Sports Illustrated,* "They couldn't sing very well, these women, but that did not matter. They sang their out-of-tune National Anthem and they were beautiful. . . . Take a picture of what you wanted to show the world about the United States, the place where we live, and this was as good as any—the U.S. women's hockey team, gold medalists, Olympic champions. . . . Women certainly can play the game—any game imaginable—and they live in an environment, a society, a country, where this is now possible."

Here was a male sportswriter acknowledging what a number of youth hockey people, from coaches to fans, had often refused to admit when I was playing the sport as a young California girl. My journey to Olympic stardom had faced numerous roadblocks, perhaps the biggest being the lack of recognition that little girls can actually grow up to excel in—and love—the game of ice hockey.

CHAPTER 2

The Birth of Ice

Me at age 2.

Above, at the party for my eighth birthday, my frilly pink dress didn't prevent me from teeing up a ball during a slapshot contest. Left, that's Pamela in front of me during our first year of ice hockey with the Conejo Hockey Club Mite C team.

I was born in California's San Fernando Valley, in Panorama City, on January 3, 1980. My family lived in nearby Sylmar, which is the kind of hard-scrabble Los Angeles County suburb where weeds popped up between the sidewalk seams, water-wise plants took over lawns, and orange poppies sprouted by the roadside. The palm fronds did not shed, but the California sycamores did—it was the only local tree that made you recognize autumn was happening. Otherwise, you estimated the seasons by the thickness of smog on the horizon. The air of August and September was the color of a corrugated cardboard box.

My dad's nickname for one house in the neighborhood was "crack in the box," since he suspected the owners of being druggies. This meant that we kids rarely got to leave the house without adult supervision. On New Year's Eve gunshots rang out as people discharged pistols recklessly into the air, and my dad made us hide under his huge desk for fear of falling bullets. On Halloween my parents' hand-selected which neighbors' houses we could approach for treats—or for the five pennies we sometimes got back then. They didn't know or trust most of our neighbors.

We lived with residential restrictions but it didn't matter to us, and Southern California had its charms. Shorts were an acceptable form of attire any day of the year. In front of our house, mom taught me to ride my bike on a 20-foot stretch of sidewalk. She wouldn't allow us to go beyond the width of our driveway. I'd peddle three times, stop, turn the bike around, and peddle three times over. Back and forth like that left little momentum for crash and burns.

For the first seven years of my life, we lived in a three-bedroom home. My younger brother Billy, my older sister Pam, and I shared one room, complete with triple bunk beds. I slept closest to the popcorn ceiling. I loved that bunk bed until the night I fell off the top and gave myself a bloody nose. From that point on I shared the middle bed with Pam. It was a cozy but comfortable arrangement. All of us were so close in age we always seemed to share the same interests at the same time. It made for less fighting and more laughing among sibling rivalries.

On sunny days (which was almost every day) we took turns getting on the backs of our Great Dane dogs, Colonel and Major, and riding them like a wild west show. At 160 pounds strong and 30 inches tall, they were eye-level with our kitchen table. When we weren't racing dogs in the backyard, we were climbing trees. I'm pretty sure Mom had nightmares about scraping me off the pavement. She would yell from out the back door for me to come inside for dinner to find me yelling back, waving at her from the very top of a tree.

Looking back at my behavior, I can see that risk-taking is an ingrained part of my happiness and livelihood. Already at the age of five, I had a proclivity for challenges. I wore pink karate pajamas and was known as "the ninja kata" by my dad. At age five I broke my leg on an exercise bike while trying to beat the recorded speed of my father's 25-year-old friend, and I played soccer and climbed trees even with a cast on my leg. I didn't want to sit around and watch cartoons. I was a kid of the sunny outdoors no matter how big or small my play world was.

By the time I was seven, my parents decided to leave Sylmar. We moved to the complete opposite end of the California

118 freeway, about 30 miles west. Deemed at the time the safest city of its size in the nation, Simi Valley, in Ventura County, became what I now consider my childhood hometown. There we moved into a house that was one of many in a tract home community. Ours was the last one on a cul-de-sac, and it had a pool. The new neighborhood was a perfect place for bike riding, soccer playing, and running. No restrictions other than a bath before bedtime. The neighborhood—chemically treated lawns, Spanish-tiled roofs, fresh flower beds, neighborhood watch signs—was the site for after-school and weekend outdoor rousing. If you flew close enough over Simi Valley at that time you'd see kids zigging and zagging in streets in front of close and evenly spaced homes.

While we lived in Simi Valley, Dad continued to commute to Canoga Park to manage his glass business. He was a business risk-taker, and like any small business, his business suffered its ups and downs. When business was booming, Mom helped out Dad, but she always had the time to take care of the kids, from when we were all in diapers at the same time (I think Dad changed each of us only once, to say that he did it) into our later years.

The financial stability allowed my parents, hoping to find the best curriculum available, to send us to private school on and off for a number of years. But periodically when money was tight my parents pulled us out of the private schools and placed us into public schools. My elementary school days were thus rather transient in nature. Kindergarten through first grade I attended Valley Park Baptist; the first part of second grade (as well as grades four through six) I attended White Oak Elementary School. But I fulfilled my latter half of second grade and all of third grade at a private school, Faith Baptist. When I first entered Faith Baptist the students had already learned how to write the cursive "L." I had not even learned an "A." The teachers held my hand until I managed to catch up. Being one step back required me to work harder than most of the other students, but the effort paid off. Sometimes success comes to those who can adapt the easiest.

When I was growing up it was hard to know what kind of person I would become because I had a father who had a son—the perfect piece of clay for a man to mold, based on his own desires—and two daughters. I think most parents want nice girls who are not promiscuous, get good grades, make curfew, have compassion for others, take an active interest in extracurricular activities, graduate from college, get married, and have babies. I doubt a suburban mother and a father from California ever dreamed that their daughter might become a female pioneer in a budding sport like women's ice hockey. Well, surprises happen.

My parents' decision to get together in the first place surprised many. Mom was born in Idaho but lived most of her life in California. Her family alone could make up a hockey team, with four sisters and two brothers. After high school she entered the army for a year. During a two-week break from the army, her major had encouraged her to apply for a position in West Point. The military academy was just starting to open up opportunities for women and he thought that, because my mom was smart and athletic, she could potentially meet its elite requirements. She also had three other options during that break: go skydiving with some friends, go to the Bahamas, or elope to Las Vegas with Bill Ruggiero. At the age of 19, she decided to lock down her relationship and pursue a family life. The marriage also allowed her an honorable discharge from the army, so her military career ended almost as quickly as it began.

My mom and dad wasted no time in starting a family. Mom had Pamela at 21 years old, me at 22, and Billy at 23. Pam and I are 360 days apart, which means that for five days out of the year we are the same age. Mom often treated us as twins, dressing us up in the same outfit, only different colors. I remember she made us frilly dresses for our joint eighth and ninth birthday party. My dress was pink, and Pam's was green. There are photographs of us shooting hockey balls and playing soccer in those dresses at the party. Another picture showed us hitting a piñata with a hockey stick. The hockey gear was evidence of my love for the game at an early stage of life.

▼▼▼

For anyone growing up in Southern California, developing a love for ice hockey was unusual. In my case, it started as an afterthought, almost by accident. Back in the 1980s, not many girls stepped on the ice in my region. And if they did, it was to be figure skaters. I can't say I ever tried pirouettes in short skirts or double axels or toe loops. Instead I went with something perhaps equally as daring but less charted: playing ice hockey.

The hockey bug was transmitted to me through my dad. He lived with a range of compulsions, or rather passions. I remember his episodic fascinations with dogs, guns, camping, motorcycles, and then hockey. Religion was also a big part of my life early on. For instance, for many years before hockey, my dad was the head of a chapter of the Gideons, the Christian group famous for distributing Bibles—you find their Bibles in many hotel rooms. We always had thousands of copies in our garage. In fact, on some of my dad's birthdays, Pam and I used to wrap up a copy and give it to him as his present—a big hit, as you can imagine.

My dad grew up in New Haven, Connecticut. But the hockey seed was planted for him when, at age 13, he started playing goalie in recreational leagues after his family moved to Florida. He was eventually a stick boy for the professional Eastern Coast Hockey League's Suncoast Suns. Around his sixteenth birthday his family moved to Southern California and he took up street hockey. He always had a thirst for the game and its culture. I remember a few times he tried to convince the family to move to Canada or to Minnesota—anywhere closer to havens of hockey. At one point he actually put a $500 down payment on a house in Duluth, but pulled out at the last minute. It wouldn't be for many years, until I'd gone off to Choate, that he'd go through with this move north, to Michigan, to help Billy's hockey career.

I think that some sports parents support their kids in an activity because they wished they could have excelled at it in their prime—the child can pursue a dream that the parent never got to pursue through his or her own childhood. For my dad, I think it was more of an opportunity to look for ways to move his love from inside himself into the hands of his kid. I cannot really say that was the case with me, at first. Billy was the target of my dad's hockey affection. Billy was being groomed to play in the National Hockey League, which is many a hockey-obsessed dad's dream for his son.

My chance came when I was seven. When Dad signed Billy up for his first hockey league, the recreational administrator at the ice skating rink in nearby Thousand Oaks asked if the family had any other children.

"I have two other kids—just girls."

"Bring them along; there's a family discount."

In Dad's eyes, now Pamela and I could become, for a small discounted price, the proud, hockey-playing sisters of our NHL-bound brother, as well as have some fun and learn a new skill. Hockey would become the sport that would bring the family together, allowing us to spend hours on end talking to each other in the car. My father therefore made hockey a family sport for all five of us to enjoy.

On my first Saturday morning in Thousand Oaks, I remember the cold of the rink when we entered the facility. At a typical rink the temperature in the stands may be in the fifties Fahrenheit, and even cooler down on the ice surface. As a Southern California kid, anything below sixty degrees buried me inside my sweatshirt for a week.

My first time at the rink, I was clueless about our mess of new equipment and uniforms, so it was up to Dad to get me dressed. As if I were three years old, I leaned on Dad's shoulder as he squatted to dress me. Each piece of gear felt like enough armor to withstand a bullet. From toes to head, he started with shin guards, hockey socks, garter belt to hold up the socks, jill (which is the female version of the hockey cup), hockey pants, neck guard, shoulder pads, elbow pads, jersey, helmet, and mouth guard. Dressing took about 15 minutes, time enough for me to shiver until each exposed body part was covered.

"Go to the ice, Ang," Dad said and slapped my bottom.

"But, Dad, I don't know how to skate," I protested.

"Go get on the ice."

"But—"

My dad walked me to the ice surface and closed the door behind me.

I felt like an astronaut except I was walking on narrow metal blades in an intense gravitational environment. Wobbly ankles. Tipsy. Exhausted from carrying fifteen to twenty extra pounds of gear just from the dressing room to the ice. Thankfully, the distribution of weight was equal. I ran my hand along the ice rink's wall, feeling my way along the outside of the boards as if blind and occupying someone else's body with terrible coordination. I wondered, are athletes supposed to feel this clumsy? Before this moment, my arms and legs and head had always felt in line with my athletic movements, whether sprinting or dribbling a soccer ball. This clumsiness took me out of my body's comfort zone. I wondered, how do hockey players ever get used to this feeling of being out-of-control in their body? Plus, if I fell, how the heck do I ever get back up with all this gear on?

Alone. Cold. Bulky. One step forward. Ice. Slip. Have you ever tried hugging a flat vertical surface? The wall became my home base during this first time on the ice. The white boards surrounding the rink couldn't have been close enough to my chest. I inched and rubbed my skates against the sheet of ice, allowing zero space for picking up my feet. And still I slipped front and back. This was going terribly. I didn't want to be here. Tears came and my mouth became slobbery from the chunky mouth guard.

I yelled out to my father from inside the rink: "I can't do this. I can't do this. I want to go home!"

But my dad would never allow us to quit at anything. He always made us try things first before giving up on anything.

With each clumsy skate around the rink, I slowly let go more and more of the boards until I became hands-free and standing up. Two hours later, at the end of practice, I didn't want to leave. I was hooked; I was skating; I was in love.

▼▼▼

For the next several years, ice continued to be four freeway interchanges away from home over the course of 40-some miles. The trip to and from the rink in Pasadena, the closest one to our house, took an hour. During the fall and winter, when we'd play a season with the Pasadena Maple Leafs, Dad always found us extra ice, twice a week, at Jack White's Hockey Basics. It was $26 a day for Billy, Pamela, and me to play. We left the house two hours before practice started in order to battle the rush hour traffic. Every day people drive 90 million vehicle miles in Los Angeles County. Our family alone was responsible for racking up many thousands of those miles in those years.

Los Angeles, dense in total driving time and see-through on dream making, allowed us time in the van to bond. Captive in that privatized space, during the late 1980s, we didn't watch movies from screens on the back of front-seat headrests or each pull out our own music headset. No, we talked, looked out the window, or sat quietly, thinking and fantasizing about the next big challenge on the ice. If our homework wasn't finished right after school, then we completed it in the car. If we didn't complete it in the car, then we finished it the next morning at school while we ate our breakfast in the cafeteria.

It was during those times that I grew intensely close to my brother and sister—a bond that we enjoy today, though thousands of miles and different life paths now separate us.

Once hockey became life, especially for Billy and me, we had few regular friendships at school, and we had hours upon hours in the van together. You'd think that with the success I've enjoyed in the sport, Billy, who now plays professional hockey in the Central Hockey League, might feel a little envious. But he remains my biggest supporter and I'm his biggest supporter, and I can trace the strength of that bond to our days of riding in the van, then playing for the same team, then riding home together. We shared those experiences then, and we share what we can of our lives now.

The civic center in Pasadena is settled among streets where palm trees arch into the sky, where flora is the fragrance, where Cal Tech students roam the streets on bikes, and where rose-petal floats parade once a year. Our rink in the center was just yards from the site of the annual Emmy Awards. The rink was actually a converted ball room, so the impressive windows on one side always let in beaming rays of light to brighten up our afternoon practices. There was also a set of gigantic chandeliers that swayed gently back and forth high above our heads.

Ice time usually lasted for 90 minutes. After practice, Dad stopped off at a pay phone to call Mom to see if he needed to pick up dinner. Normally, Mom had dinner warming on the stove when we arrived home between ten or ten-thirty at night. When she didn't cook, we picked up Chef Boy-ar-dee ravioli. I was an expert at the microwave by age nine.

Our weekend started on Friday night. While my school friends slept over at each other's house, ate pizza, watched movies, and painted their nails funky colors, I turned in early. Dad, a night owl anyway, never slept on Friday nights; he stayed up all night because he didn't want us to miss getting up at three o'clock in the morning. He'd wake us at a time when coyotes cackle and roam and bakers are kneading the day's batter.

Around four in the morning, we'd all pile into the van and drive to the rink in Pasadena. We'd arrive in enough time to put on our equipment, warm up, and then be on the ice by five-thirty for the start of practice. It was then that I became aware of a well-known fact: kids get the worst ice time. Practice lasted most of the morning, Dad directing and coaching from the sidelines in our first couple of years. Noontime meant downtime. We would head home for lunch and afternoon naps (Dad's always longer than mine) and general collapse until Sunday morning.

Dad was strict that we take this sport seriously, even if we collectively were under the age of 25. Saturday night Mom made us a championship-winning meal of pasta, pasta, and more pasta to prepare us for the next morning. Sunday morning meant more driving across the Los Angeles basin for our weekly game. We often traveled as far as Norwalk and Ontario, some 60 and 80 miles from home, respectively, just for ice and competition. I have to admit, though, it was the after-game rituals that I really loved as well as the game itself. Someone always offered us juice boxes and snacks, as the coach gave us the post-game pep talk.

We spent the rest of the week on and off the ice. Monday nights in Pasadena again and Tuesday nights in Van Nuys. Wednesdays and Thursdays were our "weekends," as in days of rest. Dad had this sixth sense for finding ice time, even if it was an hour-and-a-half away from home *and* before school started. He would call ahead to schedule the practice, with the lead: "I'd like to arrange for some ice time with my son. Is this possible?" They would invariably schedule him in and then Dad would close with, "Oh, and if it's all right, I'm going to bring my daughter, too."

In Southern California, hockey is an organized event. It takes driving to out-of-the-way locations and to where other players congregate to find ice. Players in Minnesota or Canada can, during the winter months, simply drive or walk to any one of the frozen lakes for a little free play on a whim or for a pick-up game. Plus, ice rinks are almost as common as gas stations. Not so in Southern California—during this period of my childhood, this half of the state had only about ten ice hockey rinks. When Dad did solidify extra practice time, he woke us up at four-thirty in the morning in order to play on the ice by six. I remember my fourth-grade teacher being angry with me for arriving a few minutes after the bell at eight o'clock every so often. While other kids were yawning, I was wiping the sweat from my brow.

You might think my grades foundered from this hockey fanaticism, but it actually focused my studies. I still managed to pull down straight A's in my classes; it seemed my schoolwork was totally in line with the expectations of my teachers and parents, and myself. I guess I learned time management at a young age. I've found that I actually get more done when I am busy, rather than when I have lots of time to waste.

Given this schedule, Dad gave us one week off in the summer. Here's another way of breaking it down: for 200 days out of the year, I played hockey. I probably played 1,400 days out of some 2,500 available days of my youth between the ages of seven and fourteen. This kind of dedication to the ice limits a childhood of sleepovers and movie going. To some extent

I gave up my childhood. But there should never be an age requirement for life's lessons learned. When I look at where I've been in a quarter of the average lifetime, I can only think about what I've really gained.

And I have to add that I loved hockey. Parents wondering how much they should push their kids often approach me. They wonder how much is too much. Given my own background I always have one simple answer: ask your kids and make them stick to their word. I loved hockey with a passion, but at times, like most kids, I wanted to skip practice to watch a new episode of "Saved by the Bell" or to just hang out. But, since I committed myself at the beginning of the season to my team (and to my family, which assumed a large financial burden for my sake), I rarely got to miss practice—even on Halloween. This lesson at a young age was fundamental for me. I was not allowed to quit. Ever. Still, I viewed hockey as a wonderland of sorts— I still have not grown out of it and now make a living playing it. I loved it and this is the essential component in making a great hockey player: passion and work ethic. Part child, part parent.

Looking back at this first turning point in my youth, I realize that people—especially kids—aren't always willing to push themselves to excel. Pushing becomes a new structure in life. You need a parent, a coach, a family friend to step in and show you what you don't know. Without that kind of role model it's rare in youth to have the kind of discipline to constantly polish your skills. A team sport also requires that you not only work together with your teammates, but that you push extra hard when another team matches your skill level. It is at those times that your play rises from a personal plateau to a higher level.

And for that, team sports not only support camaraderie but also individual goals.

▼▼▼

Hockey in Southern California during the mid-1980s was, for the most part, a ghost sport. It really was the beginning of girls' hockey in the United States, despite the fact that the first women's hockey game had been played almost a century earlier (in 1891, in Ottawa, Canada). In all of Los Angeles, three girls played that I knew of—Pam, Jack White's daughter Brooke, and me. USA Hockey says that fewer than two hundred girls were registered to play nationwide around the time that I began to skate.

This meant that claiming to be a hockey player was tough, particularly if you were in the second grade and relatively new to the area. Kids in my class said, "You don't play hockey. No one plays hockey here." And then they'd laugh at me. Some did not even know what hockey was. Soccer, surfing, volleyball, baseball, basketball—sure, all of these pastimes were believable. But *ice hockey?* In a somewhat unconvincing retort, I said, "Yes, I do!"

I never knew what was harder for them to believe—that some kids played hockey or that some girls played hockey. There is only so much a kid can do to win the hearts of new schoolmates. Then one day at school I had my chance to show my classmates what I had been talking about. The teacher had asked us to wear a costume that answered the question: What do you want to be when you grow up? I showed up in my hockey gear and said, "I want to be a hockey player." I didn't say that I wanted to be Wayne Gretzky, although I adored him. Just a hockey player was cool enough for me. Kids "ooohhed" and "aahhhed"; they just wanted to look at me in my equipment. Then the kid in the astronaut costume came out and stole my thunder. Although this Neil Armstrong impersonator won first place, I came in a pleasing second.

I ended up having my hockey friends and my school friends. Looking back at this split between peer groups, I think this was a lesson on diplomacy and social graces. Both groups became solid colleagues of mine as I played with them and learned from them in various arenas along the way to become the person I am today. At least from that point on in school, the kids knew hockey was real, even in Southern California.

Our family changed houses about as much as we transferred schools. I lived in nine different houses during my childhood years. In one particular instance I remember Dad had lost his job, but I didn't know why. My parents tried to shield us from financial woes. One day we had to pack up and leave our first Simi Valley house. I wasn't sure why we had to move, but I knew my parents had turned pack day into a competition. We raced to see who could throw out the most stuff (I won). Years later I heard pips and squeaks around the house about why we had to move from that house: my dad's business had failed so we had to sell our house.

After my father's business closed, I knew we had financial hardships because we received free or subsidized school lunches. My father often could not afford to pay our dues at the Pasadena ice rink. We could not afford a Christmas tree a couple of years, instead opting for a plant. I no longer got to go clothes shopping at the beginning of the school year at the mall, instead surfing the racks of the Salvation Army. There was no allowance—I made some money buying 25-cent candy bars from Pick-N-Save and selling them for a dollar at school to the other kids. We ate ramen noodles and wok-cooked concoctions of beef, corn, and rice over and over again. I never got the basketball hoop I badly wanted because we couldn't afford it.

Somehow, hockey always found a place, even in our most desperate times (which weren't, when you come right down to it, all that desperate—my parents always put food on the table). The Pasadena rink worked with my dad to help him catch up on dues. Meanwhile, we developed a tight bond with one of our coaches, Scott Plumer. Scott was my main coach from when I was 9 to 14 and was always like a big brother to me. He always watched out for the Ruggiero kids and had a heart of gold. One year, when we knew we weren't going to have any Christmas presents, Scott showed up on Christmas Eve with armfuls of carefully wrapped packages for us kids. I remember that he brought me a Los Angeles Kings (the local NHL franchise) starter jacket, boatloads of candy, and all sorts of little trinkets that made our house light up. But what I remember even more is the feeling that we hadn't been forgotten, that somehow Christmas had been saved.

When hockey wasn't helping us limp along in small ways like this, it was a safe haven for us kids. Those periods of financial difficulty naturally strained my parents' relationship at times, and Dad experienced periods of pulling deep within himself and other periods of clashing with my mother. But hockey remained the constant for him and for all of us—we continued our daily journeys, and we found this common place to grow close with my dad. On the ice, we found safety from the pressures of monetary struggles, and if there was ever any frustration we felt, it was easy to let go of it and exhaust ourselves while chasing the puck, banging into the boards, and trying to build our passing and shooting skills.

Dad's love of hockey was total—it was the one thing that never changed about him. Eventually, he even tried opening another small business called the Hockey Stop in Van Nuys. His most reliable customers, other than the psycho hockey families like us, were gang members looking for L.A. Kings hats and jerseys—they didn't show much interest in shin guards, nut cups, or sticks. This business lasted about a year and a half and then he shut the doors. I guess I learned a key aspect to my future entrepreneurial endeavors: location, location, location.

In times of despair, some people turn inwards and others turn outwards. Dad did both. What I never knew at the age of seven, where my hockey story really begins, is that my father's desire to turn his kids into hockey nuts has afforded me tremendous personal growth as well as allowed me to travel worldwide, from countries where pachinko parlors are king (Japan) to where filmmaker Ingmar Bergman is worshipped (Sweden) to where ice hockey reigns as *the* spectator sport (Canada), to name just a few. You can say I owe it all to my dad for his burning dedication to the game and to us kids . . . and to my mother for keeping this crazy hockey family together during those turbulent years.

CHAPTER 3

Getting the Girl

During my playing days at Choate, I'm protecting the puck from an on-coming player.

Top, on my right, Elizabeth Childs, my friend and teammate, and I cross hockey sticks in the locker room at Choate. Left, after my Mite B team won the 1989 Southern California and the California State Championship, I posed on the ice with the two trophies.

*A*bby Hoffman had the right hair but it still landed her in trouble. She's sort of like Gwyneth Paltrow's character Viola De Lesseps in *Shakespeare in Love,* who disguises her femininity in order to play a male leading role in a play at a time when women were not allowed to be part of an acting troupe. Well, Hoffman faced a similar act of gender discrimination in Canada during the 1950s. She cut her hair short to play on the only youth hockey league at the time in the Toronto area—a boys' league—for most of a season. This nine-year-old girl challenged the "boys only" policy in youth hockey, which led to a court case, landing in the Ontario Supreme Court. The court soon ruled against Hoffman—no girls allowed—but this policy has not stood the test of time.

Flash forward thirty-some years later, after the women's movement has made gender equality a force to be reckoned with in North America. Before games, Mom combed and pulled back my long blonde hair into a ponytail or braids that reached my butt. Hair that long became an "X" on my back for spectators and players. During our third year on the ice, Pam dropped out of hockey because of the division of ages and leagues. She had graduated to the Squirts division, while Billy and I were still part of the Mites division. Pam wanted to explore other areas in her childhood, such as music and the arts. She was going to come back and play with me when I moved up a division, but ended up staying away from the ice. Brooke was then the only other girl that I skated with, except she too was a year older and a division ahead of me. Thus, I was suddenly alone.

When I first started to play hockey, I wanted to be a goaltender, because I envied Billy's cool gear. I thought that being in the NHL and catching a puck traveling at over 90 miles per hour with those lobster-claw-like gloves would be a great rush. But Dad was grooming Billy for NHL goaltending stardom, not me. So, then I decided that becoming a defenseman was the second-best position for me. I thought this position meant you could go anywhere on the ice. Unfortunately, I found out later this wasn't the case—my teammates to this day still have to remind me that I am a defender. But I love to get involved in the rush up the ice, like the famous #4 Boston Bruins' defenseman Bobby Orr used to do. (I've long looked up to Orr—we share #4, and we both play defense though with an offensive flair.) In the end they kept me in this position because I skated backwards better than most—an essential skill to defend against an onrushing puck-carrier—and because of my size. I was a head taller than the boys and eventually became known as "the terminator." My dad always egged me on to be physical with the boys so that he could say, "That's my girl out there." I took care of myself on the ice.

At the rink before games, I went to the girls' bathroom upstairs to change into my under gear and then ran back down to the boys' locker room to finish putting on my equipment. Billy was on the team, so the boys became like brothers to me rather than strangers who might tease or taunt me because I was the only girl.

I have to say, though, that there were a number of others who did often taunt me, including not only opposing teams' players but also their parents. As I rounded the corner near the boards, checking some boys or scoring a goal, I would hear parents yell out from the stands: "Get the girl! Get the girl!"

I was a threat—taller, bigger, stronger, and more skilled than most of the boys. As the lone girl on the ice, coupled with the "C" for captain on my jersey for a few of those years, I was leading our team of six forwards, two defensemen, and Billy in goal. And some of these teammates were promising in their own right, and ended up going far in hockey. For example, defenseman Garrett Stafford would grow up to play hockey for the University of New Hampshire and for various semiprofessional teams around the country. One of our forwards, Tommy Stone, went on to play some junior hockey (sort of like baseball's minor leagues). Forward Bryan Sterling's brother Brett even went on to play for Colorado College, where in 2005 he was one of three finalists for the Hobey Baker Memorial Award, given annually to the top college player.

All along that season, as nine year olds, we knew the local championship could be ours because of our size, talent, and speed. Sometimes on the weekend, we met for off-ice conditioning at a local high school field. Our coach, Gary May, arranged our amateurish but serious routines that consisted of kicking the soccer ball, stretching, running the track for time, and playing handball. We all had boundless energy from carbohydrates, sugar, and passion for the game. Plus it was always perfect outside in California.

Winning, I've found, results from a perfect blend of ambition, determination, and luck. I first sampled this when our Pasadena Maple Leafs team won the state championship in 1990. At the age of nine I developed a fond taste for victory.

I guess it just showed me that I was naturally competitive and loved to win.

Once a year our team traveled to Colorado Springs for a Thanksgiving tournament. There I would eye my unspoken defenseman rival who played for the Colorado team: Brandi Kerns, a fellow chick on ice who also had a long blonde ponytail. There was this underlying tension between the teams and parents: *Our girl is better than your girl.* Nearly a decade later, she would lead her teammates at the University of New Hampshire to the women's first ice hockey collegiate national championship at the Fleet Center in Boston and help establish U.N.H. as *the* school to beat in women's ice hockey.

When we left Colorado Springs, I would remember Brandi as the first girl I played against outside my native California, and I would remember the first snowflakes I saw out the van window. I stuck my hand out, trying to catch one as a keepsake, only for it to dissolve. These firsts would become cherished memories in my life, although at that moment I was just looking forward to getting back to Simi Valley, where we'd spray fake snow on the windows and, hopefully, put up a Christmas tree. That was the year I wanted an L.A. Kings starter jacket, which would be too warm to wear anywhere except at the rink. The jacket represented who I was and who I wanted to become. I wanted strangers to know or at least speculate that this girl could cut ice on skates and pass, shoot, and score.

▼▼▼

I remember thinking after the Pasadena championship that success was much more memorable than failure. But I was wrong. Sometimes failures shine brighter and longer in your memory than successes, and require you to reflect longer and harder. Before my tenth birthday I became aware of the politics of gender in hockey, a lesson dealt with by almost every female player I know today that has risen through the ranks.

Billy and I had tried out for Team California, a statewide team that would travel to Canada for a select tournament. I knew I was as good as, if not better than, the others. Yet when they narrowed down the team, the coaches selected me only as a first alternate. This meant that if another player got sick or injured, I was able to play. Dad didn't even have to tell me why I didn't get on the starting lineup. I just knew: I was a girl. It was as if I didn't even make the team. First alternate was a slap in the face, an afterthought. I wanted to play.

Playing in a Canadian tournament was the scheduled highlight for the team that year. Real international play was within reach. Canada—site of the first woman's ice hockey game, birthplace to hockey greats ranging from Gordie Howe to Wayne Gretzky—was to hockey what Hollywood was to moviemaking. I wanted to trek across the cold streets, feel my blades against its frozen water, smell the clean, crisp air. Plus, this would be my first stamp in a new passport. This was the big time.

Part of me fantasized about one of my teammates getting sick or injured just so I could play. And then it happened. When Dad and Billy got to the airport to meet the team for the international flight, the coach said two players had showed up sick.

"I can get Angela to the airport within an hour and we'll still make the flight," Dad said to a coach. "She has her passport and gear ready in case I had to make this call home."

"Bill," the coach said, "That's not necessary."

"Really, she's ready and really wants to go."

"Bill, she's a girl."

I never got to go and had to hear about the team's games over the phone from my brother and dad.

This burning moment melted into a grudge that spurred me on to become an aggressive, but not a mean or dirty, player. I think this entire incident was the turning point of my becoming a better player. This strike against me in a boy's world meant that I had to be more willing than ever to prove myself each time I stepped out on the ice. Loss spurs you to action.

From that point on, when I played and heard parents shout from the stands, "Knock her down. Knock her down," it inspired me not to mow my opponent over but to out-skill and to out-maneuver him. I wanted to prove my worth every minute I was on the ice, in both practices and in the games. Adrenaline fueled my physical play as I sought to outpace the boys in the game. Sometimes though, especially in the world of checking hockey which I loved as a kid, accidents did happen. During one game, while scrambling for the puck, I inadvertently broke a boy's collarbone with a clean hit on the boards, and in another I broke a boy's leg while we checked and chased down the puck. Don't get me wrong, I'm not bragging and I don't consider these incidents some kind of badge of honor, but I mention them as evidence that I had to hold solid ground in order to continue to play. I would prove myself in all areas of the game.

By the time I hit puberty the boys were starting to parallel or surpass my size and strength. Some of them also began to use sexual taunts, like those that construction workers are famous for directing at women passing by, while we checked and skated side by side. In the summer of 1994, after playing boys' hockey for eight years, it was time for me to join my native state's first all-girls' hockey team, the CalSelects. Scott Plumer also switched to girls' hockey and helped to organize and coach our team, where the players' ages ranged from 13 to 19. Some of us had years of experience, while other girls on the team were new to the sport but demonstrated great potential. For example, Chanda Gunn, who would go on to make the U.S. Women's National Team in 2004, played in her first hockey tournament at the age of 14 with the team.

For girls, participation in highly organized club hockey often translates to educational opportunities. These clubs give girls the exposure needed to attend, participate, and showcase their athleticism to college preparatory school coaches and college coaches looking to recruit fine players for their teams. At some point, if you're serious about taking hockey to its furthest point, you have to leave the boys behind. Had I continued playing on boys' teams in Southern California, my talents might have been masked and my name unknown to recruiting coaches, especially because I would have rarely traveled outside of the state to play.

With the CalSelects I had the opportunity to travel and play in an exhibition tournament in Connecticut. This chance to play in a region heavy with prep schools became a fortuitous, life-altering event, which I wouldn't discover until a couple of months later.

During a July day before my ninth-grade year, I was on the phone with my friend Christa. The beep of call-waiting interrupted our conversation and I clicked over. It was Dad, and there was a tone in his voice of seriousness and excitement. He proceeded to tell me about an opportunity of a lifetime that had my name on it: Choate Rosemary Hall, which to me sounded like a fragrance in a fancy bottle. In actuality it was a college preparatory school in Wallingford, Connecticut, that had a reputable girls' ice hockey team and prestigious academics. Not only did the Choate coach want me to play, but so did the Connecticut Polar Bears, a nationally known girls' program. They had seen me play earlier that month at the tournament, and they later approached Dad about this opportunity.

Apparently, all those involved were doing their homework on *me*. The Choate hockey coach, Kristin Harder, and admissions counselor, Ray Diffley, checked out my grades and they passed the entrance requirements. I had never even thought of going away to prep school, but thankfully I was pulling straight A's at my public junior high school and had recently been named to the National Jr. Honor Society. Without good grades at that critical moment, my life may have gone in a completely different direction. As Oprah Winfrey says, "Luck is a matter of preparation meeting opportunity," and I was living proof. Dad reiterated that Choate was my chance for a great education, since the schools in Simi hadn't really challenged me academically.

And they wanted me! Dad needed just to hear it from me—would I go?

"Sure. Why not!"

"Great, but Ang, don't say anything to your mother just yet," he said. "We'll need to break her in to the idea."

It didn't really occur to me just then what I had agreed to. And it certainly didn't dawn on me that I'd have to leave home, my family, my friends, and my pets within a month of that conversation to become part of a completely new world some three thousand miles away from what I knew as home. At 14, I just wanted to play hockey, and anywhere that allowed me to do it sounded pretty cool. A life-changing event like this didn't come without a mild set of anxieties.

The cost of a Choate education—more than $30,000 for a boarding student—seemed daunting in itself. Where did families get that kind of money, anyway? Once my mom was sold on the idea, she and my dad assured me that Choate had a great financial aid package that wouldn't strap them to the poorhouse. I wasn't exactly sure what financial aid meant, but I knew Dad and Mom weren't worried about the money. Dad wanted me to go because, as a kid growing up in New Haven, he knew of Choate's reputation as a place where the well-heeled, smart, and college-bound went. Just as importantly, other girls my age would be there who were as serious about playing hockey as I was. It was the perfect combination.

Boarding school was a realm of private education that was new to me. I imagined it was a place for girls who wore ribbons in their ponytails and had a vast collection of argyle kneesocks. I had bet that the chicks even wore solid ties to match their plaid shirts, with that intriguing diaper-like pin on the front flap, the kind of wardrobe Britney Spears would later sensationalize in her "Hit Me Baby One More Time" video. On the other end of the spectrum I imagined those "rebel" preps that wore their shirts untucked over their short plaid skirts, smoked during lunch breaks, and had ratty hair tasseled into a faux-bun. I imagined that the boys wore typical khaki pants and collared Ralph Lauren polo shirts. But all of the boys and girls there would presumably be brilliant, rich, and Ivy-bound. I assumed that these kids were bored with their family life and took refuge knowing that their parents—who either intently watched over them or ignored them altogether—would let go and allow them to develop independence at a young age.

I wondered if I would have to turn in my hoop earrings for a strand of pearls to fit in at Choate. Plus, would I even like the cafeteria food? It was tantalizing to think about having options at every mealtime, instead of eating my family's usual wok specialty of meat, beans, and corn. Perhaps there I would have an unlimited supply of Golden Grahams any time of the day. In the morning a staff member would fill each plastic dispenser, ready for me to hit it for seconds and thirds, if I wanted, and not have to parcel out a week's supply from a small box. I could skip the main course altogether and just eat cereal if I wanted. No one would be there to look over my shoulder for a balanced diet. This sounded like my dream come true: endless Golden Grahams!

Other than a single trip to the east coast that previous summer to play against the Connecticut Polar Bears, I knew almost nothing about the region. I was a west coaster through-and-through, right down to my use of "dude" and "like" to accentuate a sentence or an absurdity in a social situation. I feared that the jargon of a teenager didn't always transcend state lines, especially among a group of students whose lineage probably included four generations worth of Ivy leaguers and family crests featuring lacrosse sticks.

▼▼▼

The month before departure to Connecticut meant deciding what to pack up and what to leave behind. No longer would Pam and I be roommates, something we'd cherished all our lives. Even when we moved into a bigger house where we could have had our own bedrooms, we decided to share. She taught me how to apply mascara and eyeliner. When the lights were off in our bedroom and after we had finished playing with the cat, we discussed boys and the girls who dated them. She led a normal life and part of me envied her for that. She had the opportunity to experiment with life, hang out in the park, spend the night at her friends, and even get into trouble once in awhile. Talking with her allowed me to live vicariously in her world of popular kids. My life was a straitjacket by comparison.

Going away to boarding school also meant not being able to share clothes any more with Pam. Prep school required certain attire—one that I didn't have. I knew the Choate dress code stated no jeans, no T-shirts, and no sweatpants. Shirts must have collars. I would have to go on a shopping spree for the right clothes that would put me "in" with the Choate students, and leave the majority of my California clothes behind. I let my dad take me shopping. Bad decision. Not really one to have a sense for fashion, he started picking up clothes that looked girly and conservative: long, floral print dresses; little blossom hats; wool plaid mini-skirts; and button-down shirts. By the end of the shopping spree he had spent five hundred dollars, which was the most I remember him spending on outfitting me other than on hockey equipment. With these clothes, I was ready for tea and crumpets, in the event girls spent their afternoons doing this somewhere on campus. I hoped I could forgo this and just play hockey outside of class time.

Going away had a further consequence: I would miss my brother. We had spent nearly eight years together as hockey buddies, racking up countless hours in the van and playing together on the ice. We were like two peas in a pod, and suddenly the security that I found in him, and vice versa, was snapped. He was ingrained in my day-to-day life of school, hockey, and car rides. He always "had my back" (watched out for me) on the ice and I had his. I suspected I would even miss the fact that I got to pick on him so much. I knew that we could always write, and in fact we did, but it would never be the same.

My family packed up the van for me the next day. I was on my way to the airport. We were all excitedly talking about everything and nothing, but you could not help but notice the lump in all of our throats. This was one of the hardest days in my life, and in the lives of my family. As we pulled up to LAX, everyone started to cry. It was not one of those "I hope no one sees me" types of crying. Rather, it was a full-out belt of sobbing. We were all there together, yet, soon I would be alone. I remember getting on the plane, and the thought of my family caused nearly overwhelming pain inside. Tears welled up over and over, and finally, I had to coach myself into thinking about what life would be like after I landed—what it would be like to play hockey with some of the better girls in the country and attend a new school.

I learned something from that painful experience: when you're moving into a new phase of life and leaving behind people and relationships, sometimes the best thing you can do is look forward. You must remember, and cherish, the past and what you're leaving behind, but shift your focus to the future and your new choice. That makes it easier to live in the present and give 100 percent to what it brings.

▼▼▼

When I arrived in Hartford with my two suitcases and hockey gear I was met by Tom Generous, a history teacher at

Choate as well as its squash coach. Mr. Generous, who would soon become almost a father figure for me, displayed the kind of openness and concern you might find a man pouring into a newfound puppy. He put my suitcases in the trunk of his tiny white car and drove me to the home he shared with his wife Diane, who was an admissions officer. It was to be my home as well during my freshman year at Choate. Normally, living with a faculty member was a senior privilege. Because I was so late to accept and register at Choate, all of the student housing was occupied, leaving me to stay with the Generous family in their house on the edge of campus.

My first impression of Choate could be summed up by the word "stately," though in truth I wasn't exactly sure I knew what that meant in terms of architecture. Just looking at the proud, red-brick buildings made me feel like I should walk with my shoulders back. (I later learned that the brick, the cornices of white stone, the Palladian windows and painted woodwork were traits of Georgian architecture.) As I filed past new faces on their way to class, I was in awe of the campus. Everything was greener, darker, and more muted than in California. I was in a new world. This wasn't the kind of place where the lunchroom and lockers were outdoors, like my school out west. I wondered if you could even find a good burrito in a town the size of Wallingford. Perhaps their specialty was New England clam chowder.

You could almost feel history as you walked through the Choate campus. You cannot pass through Choate without learning the names and contributions of James Stewart Polshek, Ralph Adams Cram, and I. M. Pei. These architects designed various campus buildings, some of which went back to the school's beginning in 1890. When you're 14 years old it's hard to fathom that the man who would become the first president of the United States traipsed through Wallingford in the 1770s. Sometimes when I walked around campus, I often wondered if George Washington had placed his footprint here before, like we were sharing the same soil (literally). This town and campus made me feel as if I were a very slowly evolving and intimidated zygote. It's enough to make you humble without even trying.

My first day at school was nerve-racking. I had that butterfly feeling in my stomach the night before. I had to figure out where I was on campus, talk to students from all over the world, and manage to juggle six classes. It helped that I had organized my classes into six neat binders. The morning light flickered through the elm and oak trees lining the sidewalks. Here I was experiencing a new region, a new shade of sunlight. The higher latitude meant the sun didn't bring out the golden highlights in my skin, as did the morning sun in L.A. On the other hand, the color green from the trees and grass enveloped you.

Looking back, I'm somewhat sheepish to admit that what worried me most on that first day, more than how well I would do in school, or even how well I would do on the ice, was how I looked. I worried about my clothes and makeup appearing just right. I feared that everyone could tell at a glance I was from Southern California, and that I would never fit it. Fortunately, it wasn't long before I realized that Choate was more about who you are than what you look like. This was the complete opposite of the world I had left.

It also wasn't long before my original worries about my appearance took second seat to a more pressing set of concerns: my grades. I came in with straight A's from my school in

Southern California yet, after only a few weeks of homework, quizzes, and tests, my teachers were telling Mr. Generous, in effect, they weren't sure I'd ever be able to graduate. One admitted that my "very basic skills" in English, math, and grammar were lacking and needed a tremendous lift to become on par with my classmates.

Mr. Generous hid these first teacher comments from me, not wanting to discourage me. It wasn't until years later that he showed them to me, yet I knew that I was struggling at the time because I could not comprehend a lot of the reading in English class. Also, when asked to conjugate a verb in a French class, I responded, "I don't even know how to do that in English." I knew that I needed to put the extra time in if I wanted to graduate from this kind of school. Long gone were the days of doing my homework in the morning before class.

At the end of my freshman year I was given the award for "earnest and persistent effort," annually given to a boy and girl in each class for their effort in the classroom . . . proof that I was trying my hardest, despite the academic barriers that were in front of me. As in hockey and life, "patience and perseverance have a magical effect before which difficulties disappear and obstacles vanish," as John Quincy Adams put it. I struggled over and over my freshman year, but kept working towards the future. I knew everything would turn around in time, because somehow for me, it always did.

▼▼▼

One other thing was a redeeming factor at that point—hockey. At Choate I faced the familiar situation of being the biggest girl on the ice. Coming from California, where swimsuits and tank tops are common year-round, it didn't take a fool to know that I wasn't petite, or a girl who could fit into the hippest snug styles. I had a thick, athletic physique thanks to genetics, animal protein, and weight training. I abandoned the notion that my thighs could ever be pencil-thin or that lettuce would provide all the nutrition I could possibly need.

My physique made me stand out both on the ice and on campus, even though in Connecticut you can cover yourself up most of the school season (in California everyone sees your shape any time of the year—the weather there doesn't allow you to hide anything). One reason I stood out was because skinny was in at Choate—too skinny, in many cases. Eventually, I came to know girls with eating disorders—bulimia and anorexia were the popular choices of starvation—on campus. These are primarily diseases of the white and rich. With no parental guide eyeing their plates each evening, girls would simply skip meals. I watched in wonder as my friends got smaller and smaller, while I got bigger and bigger. I am not sure how I managed to be in the group of girls that did not obsess about their weight—perhaps it was my Olympic dream.

Along with my fellow girls on the ice, I needed all the calories I could get for practice and training. My teammates weren't dieting all the time but even so a few were quite small. I quickly learned that a nudge from my shoulder could sail a 110-pound girl into the boards. I had to leave behind my world of hard checking with the SoCal boys. In women's hockey, unlike the men's, there is no body checking allowed. You can have contact, but you cannot just lay someone out at center ice, like you see in ESPN highlights. Women's ice hockey is a game of finesse that mimics the way the Europeans play. It is based on skill, speed, and the right touch. I guess that this part of the game can either turn hockey fans away from the women's game, or turn them into die-hard fans of it. I like to think that our brand of hockey is more enjoyable to watch because there are not as many stoppages of play from penalties, and the puck is constantly moving.

I think that my size and my aggressive style of play were factors in why I usually led the Choate team in penalty minutes. When I started to play girls' hockey for the first time, where and how the flight of the player's body might react to my style of physical play meant the difference between being charged with a penalty or not. I had to learn how to hit while simultaneously holding up the player—if I knocked her over or she fell I'd likely get a penalty. If a player took a run at me and fell, I was usually the one who had to spend two minutes in the penalty box. There was a sense of dance, a suspension and release, with the movements in girls' hockey that I hadn't learned before. It was more skill-based than size-based. Basically, I started to realize that skills such as shooting, passing, and skating would help me succeed, as opposed to brute strength.

I also think that there's something of a double standard about females exhibiting aggression. In hockey, or any sport really, you might come across as being brutish or masculine. Some people see my aggressive style of play on the ice and mistakenly assume that I am mean-spirited off of the ice. Rather, I am just extremely competitive . . . and usually bigger than opposing players. It is hard for most refs to call the women's game because of this difference. They have to judge a player's intentions and not necessarily the contact. Sometimes everything is called in games, and other times, nothing at all.

Many people think of hockey as an intense, violent, physical game, which indeed the most visible (the National Hockey League, assuming the impasse between players and owners that led to the 2004–2005 season being canceled ever ends) version is. Some players in the NHL cross the line of brutality, leaving the sports channels and highlight reels fascinated with the exhibition of dirty play. When the caliber of play goes down, the fists and cheap shots come out.

This is the milieu of professional men's hockey that my brother plays in. But this is not the kind of play the majority of hockey players participate in, especially when women play. Girls don't become goons on the ice. And just because our style of play doesn't succumb to gloves being thrown off and fists flying doesn't mean it's not as aggressive or as physically demanding as men's hockey. You have to learn to skillfully separate the opposing player from the puck—the point of checking—as opposed to just hitting her to get the puck. I've noticed that many people do not even realize, when they're watching, for example, a U.S. versus Canada women's hockey game, that there is no checking allowed, because of the physicality. I love this part of the game and it has certainly made me more dominant within it, but I don't think it is needed in our brand of hockey. In international tournaments like the Olympics, sportsmanship rules and clean play is part of the game—for both men and women. Most fans have probably never seen a fight in any level of international hockey, men's or women's: it is just not part of the international experience.

▼▼▼

When I wasn't playing on the Choate squad, I played for the Connecticut Polar Bears during my freshman through junior years, and we won the national championship all three years. Playing on the club team was an opportunity to play hockey almost year-round and with the best girls in the state, and the country for that matter. The Connecticut Polar Bears, just like Choate's team, prides itself on not only the girls' level of hockey play, but their academics as well. It bases much of the organization's success on its girls' college admissions record. Players in my graduating class and those who came after me have gone on to hockey and academic careers at Harvard, Yale, the University of New Hampshire, Dartmouth, Boston College, Northeastern, Cornell, St. Lawrence, Colby, Middlebury, and the University of Connecticut. Many of the teammates I had during my years of play with the Polar Bears advanced to higher levels of hockey, including Jessica Tabb, who played for Providence College; Jamie Hagerman, Pam Van Reesema, and Julie Chu for Harvard; Jen Richardson for Boston College; Catherine Elkins for Middlebury; Courtney Johnson and Kim Insalaco for Brown; Nicole Kirnan for St. Lawrence; Lisa Giovenelli for Northeastern; and Liz Macri and Jen Wiehn for Dartmouth. Several others went on to play in the National Women's Hockey League (NWHL) as well.

Since my dad was no longer driving me to and fro, I had to depend on other parents to take his place. I remember calling the Chus, Johnsons, Venters, Swiderskis, or Tabbs to pick me up for Polar Bear practices and games. I really owe a ton to these devoted parents who would usually go out of their way to help out a kid from California. I had no clue where they were coming from in the state, but I guess it was hard to say no to a young girl's voice from her dorm room, just begging to go to practice after a long day in the classroom.

The high school and club sport programs were essential for my own development at that time, and their emphasis on educational as well as athletic excellence has grown stronger since I left. More than ever, high school athletes and club sports groom girls for collegiate and professional teams. A good program should never place the sport above core educational values. As any athlete knows, her body is her best friend and her worst enemy on any given day. You never know when that first or final injury completely takes you out of competition. A sound education allows you always to have a backup plan when (not if) your body decides one day that your time is up in the sport. And while it's true that a man's career will end early in his life, it's currently also true that a woman's career will end even sooner. Education is not only essential for the building of the whole person, it prepares individuals for life after athletics, which will be the majority of most athletes' lives.

▼▼▼

At the end of my freshman year, with finals one week away, I flew to California for a crucial tryout, leaving just enough time to get back to Choate with three days left to take my finals. Evaluators at these tryouts hoped to find overlooked players— those they might not have heard of or have seen play before. This was the central meeting place for girls who might fall through the cracks. It was designed to see the girls who were not yet on USA Hockey's radar. It was my chance to show the national coaches and evaluators my talent.

I spent the next three days going through drills and scrimmages with about 40 other women. I was the youngest one there, but I was the only one selected by Val Belmonte and USA Hockey to get an invite to a USA Hockey camp that summer. I was beside myself. The summer before I had tried out at our regional camp and had been told that I was too young to attend. This time they made an exception for me.

▼▼▼

There's a strange symmetry to how life works out sometimes. After taking my finals at Choate, between that initial tryout and hockey camp, I went home to California. Billy had continued to dominate in his league play in California, and the state was putting together a California Select team that would travel to Manitoba, Canada, to play in the Brandon Tournament of Champions, much like the team that had gone to Canada when I was nine years old. Incredibly, despite the courting I was receiving from USA Hockey, another California coach didn't want me . . . it was as though I were nine years old all over again.

This time, my father was emboldened by the player I had become. No longer was I just another Ruggiero next to Billy who happened to play pretty good hockey—I was powerful in my own right, and I had shown that I could play with boys and girls alike. Dad told the coach, "If you don't take Angela, you don't take Billy either," which would have robbed them of their star goalie.

They took me. And good for them, too—I was also the first girl to ever play in this tournament! They played me at forward because they thought that I would do the least damage there. I'm sure that much to the coach's surprise, I ended up leading the team in goals and points (goals plus assists) for the whole week and came up with clutch plays during a few key situations.

For me, in the middle of the Olympic buildup, it could easily have been a small incident compared with what I was then undergoing. But it meant more to me than that. I had been in a place much like that previous humiliation when I was young. My father had gotten me in a good position, and I had validated him, myself, and girls in general by performing.

And maybe more significant for me, though I didn't realize it at the time, it was the last time I would skate with my brother as a teammate until I was in my twenties and already through two Olympic Games and four years of college. If this small tournament had broken a few barriers and changed a few people's attitudes, our next time together would be far more significant.

▼▼▼

From the players ages 18 and under who were selected to attend the summer camp at Lake Placid, officials were going to select 20 to go on to play with the first ever women's Junior National Team in Ottawa. As I walked Lake Placid grounds, observing the Olympic rings, I felt the same awe as I had experienced at Choate. I thought of the Olympians who had walked on the very ground here before me. As any teenager would, in respect for the moment, I snapped as many pictures as I could. In some of them, I even posed myself. I remember Brandi Kerns, the girl I used to play against in Colorado, and I wore our jerseys in the locker room and took pictures of this moment, in those historic stalls, because we never expected to get that space or time back. In a sense we were daydreaming and playing dress up in the men's ice hockey memory. The presence of hockey lore haunted the room as the roster of the "Miracle Team" echoed in our heads.

When I returned after the team went 2–0–1 versus the Ottawa Select Team, I was greeted by my family as usual at the airport. It was always such a warm welcome, both literally and figuratively, coming home to my family in California. I was back on the ice a couple of days later with Billy, participating in a men's league. One morning my father told me just before practice that I needed to wear my official U.S.A. off-ice uniform. It was a track suit that we wore the week that we were in Ottawa. I loved the thing to death, but I was embarrassed to wear it, being self-conscious as any 15-year-old would be. I thought people might think that I was showing off, so I got into an argument with Dad. After a heated battle, Dad won, of course, and I stomped away and put my hockey bag into the back of the van. I was mortified.

When we got home that day, all I wanted to do was to rip off the suit and take a nap from the early skate. Little did I know that the family had planned a surprise party for me. "Surprise!!" people screamed as I walked through the door. Everyone I knew was there—my coach Scott Plumer, my hockey friends, and even a few schoolmates that I had stayed in contact with over the past year. I was floored. I guess the only giveaway that I had was the fact that Mom had bought cases of soda and chips. When I asked her the day before about them, she just shrugged them off as being "on sale." It was the perfect response.

Two weeks after leaving Lake Placid and making the Junior National Team, I went back home to California for the summer and received a letter in the mail that would change the course of my young life once again.

CHAPTER 4

Training to Become a Hockey Woman

My best friends Maria Palomar-Nebot (on the left) and Danielle Salvaterra (in the middle) at the Choate prom in 1998.

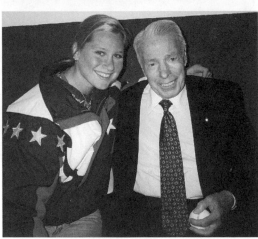

Above, that's me waving the hat on opening day at Yankee Stadium in 1998, where the women's 1998 gold-medal-winning team was feted. Left, I also got to meet Joe Dimaggio!

*I*t might as well have been 1891. In February of that year the Canadian *Ottawa Citizen* newspaper published a story about two unnamed women's teams playing in a hockey game. Hockey historians regard this as the true beginning of women's ice hockey. For me, my true beginning in women's hockey—no longer girls' hockey—happened in the summer of 1995 when I held in my hand a letter with Team USA letterhead inviting me to try out that summer for the 1996 U.S. Women's Select Team. This team was expected to constitute the core group of players who would make up the roster of the 1997–1998 U.S. National Women's Team and the 1998 Olympic Team.

Here I was still 15 years old and no longer a girl, really. I had the chance to become a woman well before any legal document told me otherwise. The Select Team recruiters had seen and chosen seven other juniors and me at the junior national camp weeks before. In women's hockey, because the talent pool is relatively smaller than the men's, if you've got talent and access to opportunities to show that talent, then important evaluators, recruiters, and coaches will notice you. They will come to you if you just show up and play at the right places at the right time, particularly at major girls' tournaments.

The letter stated that USA Hockey would fly me out for the week and a half of training camp at Lake Placid. Just the prepaid flight to the camp felt like they treated me as a professional athlete already. In a pool of 40 players, only 6 spots for defense were available. During that time period they would make a decision about how each player played and what a player's potential was.

▼▼▼

When I finally suited up and hit the ice at the training camp, I realized that my game needed acceleration in numerous points to keep up with these women. Everyone I had played against up until that time in Lake Placid didn't really compare. When it was my turn off the ice, I watched intently and vowed to emulate the good players as quickly as possible.

In addition to the obvious differences in size and speed, wisdom on the ice was the major difference between girls' and women's playing styles. These women plotted future moves well before the puck ever made its way to their sticks. More than anything, these women knew they had options and they kept many of them open. In a split second they would engage in the moment and move the puck. I had never seen such fine control over unscripted situations, whereas in my girls' world of play, we received the puck first and then looked around for options. As a result we held onto the puck longer and didn't pass until we were really sure to make a good one, all of which slowed the game down considerably. These women had several good options, never just one. Soon after the beginning of camp, I finally internalized this observation enough to start moving the puck at a greater pace to match the speed of women.

At the end of the camp, the coaches invited us women and girls into a dimly lit training room next to the Olympic Rink, filled with rows of long, slender tables and chairs. Gold Olympic rings on the wall looked back at us. It was the same training room that the 1980 Olympic men's hockey team must have used. Individuals shifted weight from side to side, sat quietly, or chewed nails. I stood in the back of the room, both to hide my anxiety and to make a quick escape, whether hearing my name or not. At 15, I was one of the youngest players there; many of the women had already graduated from college, were living adult lives, or were playing on collegiate hockey teams. I told myself, if I did hear my name called, to remain calm and not emit any girlish pig squeals or clap my hands. And definitely no dancing in place. Around this group of women, collectedness ranked higher than emotional displays.

They announced "Ruggiero" among the last names of 21 players selected. I was so excited and could barely contain myself. We were told to give our passports to the general manager so that he could process them for our trip to Finland, where we would play our Finnish counterparts in a four-game exhibition series the following week. Not only was I making the team, but I was also traveling overseas for the first time.

I waited for Coach Smith to finish his comments to all of the players. I felt truly bad for the players that did not make the cut this time, especially some of the veteran players who had helped to establish women's hockey. I was coming onto a team that had years of experience and heart and was therefore benefiting from the many women who had sacrificed to put the team on the map. I was ready to conquer the world with 20 other women. I had my family, coaches, and now the women who had come before me to thank.

I snuck out the back door as soon as Coach Smith was through. I raced to the first pay phone I saw and dialed home. My dad picked up. With a solemn voice he asked me, "Did you make the team?" I replied with a sad voice, "No." My dad did not say a word, no doubt trying to come to terms with the idea that his 15-year-old was not quite good enough. Then after a few seconds of holding it in and acting my age, I blurted out, "Just kidding. I made it!" My dad was shocked and started to scream to Billy, Pam, and my mom. I could hear them in the background shouting and screaming. They were so happy for me and I wish they could have been with me to give me a hug. My mom asked if I was happy that she had rushed to have my passport issued, after I had told her not to pay the extra money because "I'm not going to make the team anyway." Thank God that my mom had faith in me. I had received my passport the day before.

My dad had given me a one-dollar bill to use to buy myself a congratulatory soda if I made the team. He had taped it inside my helmet. I decided that it was my good-luck dollar from then on and kept it there instead of giving it away to some machine. To this day, my lucky dollar bill is still up there inside my helmet.

We went to Finland for a week and I got to play some great hockey. I had my first assist as a Team USA player. Cammi Granato, already a star player who had set goal-scoring records at Providence College, told me that on my very first shift in a USA jersey, she turned around just before the face-off and looked back to see me with a smile that stretched from ear to ear. I was just a pup, as they called me, ready to relish every little experience possible.

Most of these players and I would go on to play in various national select tournaments around the world, taking the silver in the 1996 Pacific Rim Tournament (which Canada won) and gold in the 1996 Select series against Sweden. In the spring of 1997 we took another silver (again losing to Canada in the gold medal game, this time in overtime) in the Women's World Championship and then went on to finish with a 24–7–1 record on the pre-Olympic tour in the summer of 1997.

▼▼▼

Between our travels, Billy and I decided, for the sake of both our hockey careers, to join exercise forces. Off-ice training is critical to a player's success—you want to be as strong as possible when you hit the ice for the season, because once the season starts, most of your training is on the ice and there is less time for full-body strengthening. The intensity of off-ice training does have at least one amusing effect. My teammates and I have always joked that we have two sizes of pants—a larger size during hockey season and a slimmer size for the off-season. Off-ice training tends to slim down your body, as it gets stronger, while on-ice skating during the season tends to build up your thighs and butt. The bottom line, so to speak, is that we have bigger butts during the season.

During my pre-Olympic training period, Billy was training to play in the Ontario Hockey League. We decided to get creative with the strength and endurance portion of our workouts. For example, we would finish by going to a parking lot and pushing a car that we placed in neutral for intervals of 15 to 30 seconds. We would place our hands on the chrome bumper and then, focusing on the parking lot's black pavement and yellow stripes, sprint until our legs felt the burn. I imagined that most other teens spent their summers driving cars rather than pushing them. Otherwise, girls my age, if they were spending time in a parking lot, were likely to be wearing bikinis, holding up hand-made signs, and screaming at passersby to pull over for a car wash.

Billy and I joined a gym and worked out for two hours a day that first summer of 1995, a regimen we picked up again for the next few years. We also skated, skated, skated. I think it is in our veins and to this day we skate as much as possible in the summers. I always say that I would rather get my sprints done on the ice than off the ice. Sometimes that was not possible because of a lack of ice time, so we did explosive weight training like the "clean," in which you bring a set of barbells up from the floor to your shoulders in a squatting position, to make us quicker and stronger. For such lifts, I usually warmed up with 95 pounds and worked my way up to 155 pounds over the course of five to six repetitions at four sets.

My coach also prescribed various plyometric exercises, which involve leaping and bounding. The idea is that the exercises closely resembled those movements that I encountered during competition. I also used a lateral slide board, a Plexiglas surface that enabled me, while wearing my tennis shoes, to stride like a hockey player traveling down the ice. With legs slightly bent I worked my quadriceps as hard and as fast as I could for a targeted time, remembering to keep my form and position, as if gliding across the ice. We usually did 30 seconds on and a minute off, for 10 to 12 repetitions on the slide board.

Off-ice conditioning also focused on the abdominal region, the core of a player's strength, along with the legs. I performed several different ab techniques, working the various range of muscles in that area, some exercises with a medicine ball and others without. Usually I left the session having completed 200 sit-ups and/or crunches.

And last, in Lance Armstrong fashion, I rode the stationary bike for a conditioning and cardiovascular workout. This part of the workout started with anaerobic training: eight to twelve times in a row, with active periods of rest, I sprinted for 30 seconds on the bike's high-resistance setting. Other days I sprinted on the bike for 16 minutes, which was grueling, grueling, grueling.

My legs never collapsed out from under me after I climbed off the bike, but they often came darn close.

A workout focused on the legs is never an enjoyable experience, and off-ice conditioning differs somewhat from regular season training. Often I wanted to quit because it simply hurt so badly. Some days, when my muscles were really tired, I slowed down the pace. More than anything, I needed to work on the mental aspect of my workout. It helped that I trained with my brother, but sometimes I needed to learn how to manage the pain of strength training and conditioning alone. This would come with time, I thought.

▼▼▼

From that point forward, I knew I had to just muddle my way through the pain and sweat in order to play with the women who would make up the National Team. If those other ladies could perform this workout routine, I wasn't about to back down from that challenge. As far as I was concerned, age was just a number and we all had the same chances of making the Olympic team in 1998. Perhaps my naiveté aided in this perspective. It was a matter of who wanted it badly enough, I thought. Coach Smith didn't strike me as a guy who played favorites. Everyone on the team desired to be there, and I knew the tryouts were going to be close across the board.

My dedication to training and bulking up soon enabled my strength and speed on the ice to match those of women sometimes five or ten years older than me. One particular highlight of my first year on the Select Team came during the Pacific Women's Hockey Championship held in Vancouver, British Columbia, during the first week of April 1996. At one point during the game against Japan, I rushed down the ice from the red line and shot the puck from the boards, beating Japan's goalie and scoring. This splendid moment was my first goal on the National Team. In the locker room after the game, the coach presented me with the puck, a tradition for someone's first goal.

The success didn't stop there in my young career. In 1995–1996 I still played for the Connecticut Polar Bears, who went on to win the Women's Peewee National Championship. Here I was a Select National Team player yet also playing in my club team's 15-and-under division. During those games with the Polar Bears I was the biggest girl on the ice; if someone skated into me, it was like hitting an igloo. I remember when Krissy McManus, one of my good friends, ran into me. She hit me with all five feet of her frame; needless to say, I got the best of her. I still apologize to this day and jokingly tell her that I am sorry, but she ran me!

In addition to the size difference, I was happy to be among my peers when I returned to Choate and the Polar Bears. I had forgotten how great it was to be among a crowd of cohorts who squealed, cheered, and danced in the locker room like I did. Country Western was preferred in the USA locker room and this Cali kid was usually blasting some techno bite or the latest Snoop Dogg tune.

▼▼▼

Eventually all of my training, the pushing of cars in parking lots and the hours spent pedaling on the stationary bike, and all of the ice time, whether practicing with my Choate teammates or playing against topnotch international competition, paid off when the Women's National Team won Olympic gold in Nagano in 1998. The years since then have confirmed for me that the 1998 Winter Olympic Games were a landmark in women's hockey and women's athletics. While the U.S. Women's Soccer Team's championship at the 1999 World Cup revolutionized how the country as a whole looked at women's athletics (who can forget Brandi Chastain's game-winning penalty kick, and her bra-revealing celebration?), the 1998 women's hockey gold medal did something similar, also in a sport associated mostly with men (though we kept our jerseys on). The roots of women's ice hockey had long been growing, but the 1998 gold medal thrust the game into the American media spotlight as it had never been before and gave young players for years to come something to play for.

During the 1998 Winter Olympics closing ceremony, as we made our way through the long, dark tunnel with the light of the stadium at the vanishing point, I hoisted Alana Blahoski onto my shoulders. The ceremony left behind the pomp and circumstance of the opening ceremony, where everyone stood in straight lines, held their flag, and gently waved to the world. After three weeks of play and emotion in Japan, raucous athletes filed onto the field and egged on the crowd to make noise. You train for four years to stand in that moment, which dissipates all too quickly. Hours later all that remains are personal and public memories. It didn't last long enough, but perhaps that was also a part of the moment's magic.

▼▼▼

Looking back to the 1998 Olympics, I think I was too young to truly appreciate the entire experience. It was more emotional than meaningful. Grabbing the American flag and skating around the rink has been something symbolic for many people—to me at the time, it was just the over-exuberance of victory and my youth. I am not sure I realized the significance of that victory until years later, after our team had struggled to win another international event. In retrospect, I can now appreciate the way Lisa Brown-Miller, Cammi Granato, Karyn Bye, and Sandra Whyte felt. They were the veterans and the ones who had helped establish Team USA from the beginning. Thanks also to Kelly Dyer, Cindy Curley, Erin Whitten, and countless other women hockey players who had been in their prime before the Olympics were open to the sport. They were instrumental in showcasing the game to the International Olympic Federation when it was deciding if women's hockey would be a sport. Walter L. Bush, Jr., former president of USA Hockey, and Bob Allen, who the USA Women's Player of the Year is now named after, were also fundamental in getting our sport to the highest sporting level. They pushed and pushed the International Ice Hockey Federation to include the girls at a time when the sport was barely on the map. Change is always hard and especially hard when the "girls" are asking to be part of the "old boys" club. The IIHF was reluctant at first, but the first Women's World Championship, held in Ottawa in 1990, had more than 10,000 fans in the stands to see the women play.

In some respects, like a gifted child in elementary school, I was isolated, but not in the homesick or depressed kind of way. If there is an upside to isolation it's an island of time and space you've figured out how to carve in your life in order to hone your skill and excel at what you really want. Some call it selfishness while others call it following your passion. I was also lucky that Coach Smith and USA Hockey believed in my potential and gave me a chance to hone my skills and be pushed with the big girls. Being picked at such a young age became sort of like a self-fulfilling philosophy—I had to live up to expectations. Coach Smith has always been like a great leader to me . . . and to the rest of the team. As Sam Walton said, "Outstanding leaders go out of their way to boost the self-esteem of their personnel. If people believe in themselves, it's amazing what they can accomplish." He's also noted, "High expectations are the key to everything." My sights were set high early in my hockey career and I intended to follow through with them. It was relatively easy, however, because I was following a passion. When you follow your passion, though, life doesn't seem as difficult as trudging through the muck of figuring out your life's duty. I guess I happened to figure out my passion at a young age, was pushed to excel, and perhaps that alone places me farther along on my nontraditional career choice.

Yes, I was part of a team that experienced the moment of winning. But I cannot shake the feeling that these women beside me felt different levels of accomplishment when singing the national anthem. I realized the Olympics was really the beginning of my hockey career, while some might think competing in such an event was the pinnacle of an athlete's career. Granted I had been playing for more than ten years, but the gold medal symbolized what women in ice hockey were now capable of. It opened the doors of the sport to the world and put it on a new level. We had made it. The Olympics had made us.

You cannot help but feel different from your peers when you're given a gift—mine being athleticism—at so young an age and are able to achieve the heights of the Olympics. I realize most people don't even know the first thing about what it takes to make an Olympic team. Filing a federal appeal for a legal case probably seems more logical and tangible than trying out for the Olympics.

The medal signified that I was just beginning to play real hockey, whereas some of my teammates found that it was their last endeavor in women's hockey, retiring soon thereafter to engage in a fully equipped adult life of careers, relationships, and motherhood. As far as I was concerned I was still young and prouder than ever of it. I loved the medal just as much as my other teammates, but I realized that others had paved the way for me and that they had put their time into the sport in order to carve a path for me. I came into this sport at the right time and the right place. My dad always said that I was lucky to be playing hockey because it gave me an opportunity that few other sports could provide at my age. Women's hockey was just hitting the NCAA level as well, and other universities were now pushing the "Big Three"—Providence, U.N.H, and Northeastern. In the past, before there was a National Collegiate Athletic Association (NCAA) title to shoot for, women's hockey was dominated by the Eastern Collegiate Athletic Conference (ECAC). The ECAC's title had been solely dominated by these three and by Brown and Dartmouth in the Ivy League. Because of the 1998 win, many more colleges have since added women's hockey to their athletic departments—there are now 29 NCAA Division I institutions and 43 Division III schools. That means that there are numerous scholarship schools available and many more on their way. This growth in the game has been largely due to the exposure of the Olympics. We made it, but we sure have a long way to go.

When you start laying a path, you never realize the implications of each stepping-stone you need to build the new route. Though you've trained for this moment your entire life, you can never be sure that it would actually lead to something like this: a gold medal. I was one of the first women to make ice hockey history. At the age of eighteen, I wondered what else life had in store for me. Or rather, what did I have in store for my life? The older I get the more I believe that you have to make life happen *for* you, not wait around for life to happen *to* you. You must be an active participate in seeing it through to a goal. This philosophy would become the backbone for my college experience.

CHAPTER 5

Crimson Calling

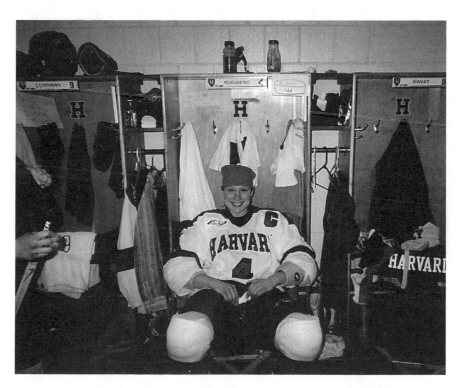

In 2003, I'm in front of my locker stall at Harvard.

Above, from left to right, that's Angie Francisco, Jen Botterill, Claudia Asano, me, and Kyle Walsh after our Harvard team won the collegiate national championship in 1999. Left, I've hoisted Jen Botterill up onto my shoulders at Niagara Falls, during a 1999 road trip.

Given the rivalry in women's hockey between the U.S.A. and Canada, our victory in the sport's inauguration as an Olympic event was simply amazing. The glow from winning in Nagano didn't fade for months. I guess what made the medal so special for us was that it was a first. There were no former Olympians on the team. No women hockey players had endured a limelight like that before. In that respect, we were all on an equal playing field. To experience a "first" as a team heightened our camaraderie.

After the Olympic Games, Team USA flew to Hawaii for a week of relaxation in the sun and surf. I ended up with the worst sunburn of my life, but at the time I didn't care. That sun offered my winter-white skin the kind of blistering you're totally unaware of as you sit in the balmy breeze and request more fruit drinks. The sunsets were accompanied by dolphins breeching on the horizon. In addition to working on my tan I fell in love with a new fish dish: mahi mahi.

This trip was a relaxation way station, our decompression chamber before we went our separate ways to enjoy hometown parties and to endure media appearances and interviews. It was also a farewell shindig, because we would all be leaving for home after most of the team had spent the past half-year with one another. For a matter of weeks, we were told, we would be treated as celebrities. In Nagano my first "celebrity" appearance after the gold medal game happened on the David Letterman show. We taped a "Top 10" list of benefits from winning the gold medal. I came in at number three with, "You get to take slap shots at the Spice Girls." My favorites in the list were number ten, when Colleen Coyne said, "Fun to set off an airport metal detector, then say, 'I'm sorry—that must be my Olympic gold medal,'" and Vicki Movsessian's number four, "Now that you have proven you are the best, you can sit on your ass and watch TV." Funny thing is, there was an element of truth in Colleen's jest. Leaving Japan, airport security searched our bags and extracted a gold medal. You didn't have to speak Japanese to understand the pleasure those attendants got as they called over their comrades, smiling and nodding and holding and ogling the coveted gold, a symbol of superior competition no matter what country you're from.

▼▼▼

My time off seemed luxurious and drawn out, and yet it also ended quickly. When I returned home to Michigan, Harrison Township had posted a sign that read "Home to Angela Ruggiero, 1998 Olympic Gold Medalist." But soon it was back to school. Choate threw me a "welcome back and congratulations" assembly and gave me a standing ovation when I walked to the center of the auditorium in my Team USA uniform with my gold medal around my neck. As I stood there among my peers, friends, and faculty, I thought what an odd juxtaposition this was from just a couple of years before when I was nearly kept from playing on the California Select boys' team. Here an entire school was lauding me as an Olympic hero who helped establish a piece of women's sports history, and in California I had been just some stubborn chick who wanted to play hockey.

I learned about that year's "Headmaster's Day." Each year the headmaster selected one day for students to have off. He had chosen the day of our gold medal game. He opened up the assembly hall and set up a big-screen television for the broadcast at six in the morning for anyone at Choate to watch the game. At a boarding school like Choate, students come from all over the world for a first-class education and to share their talents. They give over, or rather give up, a family home life for one initially filled with strangers but who, over the course of four years, become the people you know best. I showed them my talent on television and in return they showed me their capacity to support one of their own, even if it was early in the morning for high school students.

The last semester in high school I hung up my skates for a few months and focused on life as a student and track athlete. I set a New England Prep Record in the shot put and ended up winning the New England title in the shot and javelin for the third straight year (I had tried lacrosse my freshman year but then was recruited by Mr. Harder to try track). I also threw the discus. My senior year I was captain of the team and helped it to win the New England track and field championship. It was my first prep school title—my hockey team had come up just short all three years that I was there, but it was in track that I finally got a medal. Ironic, don't you think?

I spent that spring hanging out with my best friend, Maria Palomar-Nebot, a Spanish girl I had met my junior year. We talked about everything for hours on end and were even accused of being drunk a few times because we were so silly together. She never cared that I was a hockey player and took the liberty to embarrass me when NBC came to Choate to interview my friends and me. I was going to miss her and our crazy times.

I finished my English class and took a creative writing course, a sculpting class, and an acting class. You could say

I had the ideal senior year. The administration even waived a few electives I was supposed to take so that I could graduate with my friends of four years.

By the end of March, I received my college acceptance letters. When I returned from Japan, I had gone on several college recruiting trips. Dartmouth, Brown, and Harvard were at the top of my list. These institutions wanted me to play hockey as well as excel academically. When I visited Dartmouth, it felt like Choate—home—lodged deep in the woods of New England. The transition would be minimal, I thought. Then one morning while eating breakfast in the Choate cafeteria, as I was trying to make my final decision, Mr. Generous sat down next to me. He was very instrumental in steering me toward an experience outside my comfort zone. He said to challenge myself; to take a chance on the unknown. By all accounts Boston and Harvard intimidated the hell out of me, because I was just an above-average B student. While I might excel in certain aspects, I still felt a tinge of mediocrity in my life. I considered myself fairly well-rounded, but I believed the kids at schools like Harvard excelled academically far beyond my capability.

Only Mom was working at that time, and her salary alone wouldn't cover a year's tuition. She was supporting the entire family again. So, based on my family's financial situation, Harvard offered me a financial aid package and a spot in its incoming class. Harvard isn't an opportunity you skip when it's handed to you. Plus, A. J. Mleczko, my Team USA teammate, was returning for her senior year there on the hockey team. I won't say she persuaded me to attend Harvard, but she did dispel some of the legendary myths about super-competitive students—she'd never heard, for example, of a student actually tearing pages out of a library book to prevent others from reading them before a test. On the ice hockey team alone, the players were about more than sticks and skates. Some were poets. Some were valedictorians. And some were better hockey players than students. When I met the team I was certain that this was the place for me. My future teammates made the decision easy.

My entire family arrived in Connecticut for my graduation. This was Dad and Billy's first time to Choate. I drove them around that day, showing off the campus and the places I had lived my life for the past four years. Pointing to the Meeks House or the Pratt House was only so effective when trying to convey my memories. When you're away for so long and hardly see one another, your relationship takes on a positive spin. You don't say the things really on your mind, resonating deep in your gut. But you use the time you have to be pleasant and congenial, reminding them what a well-mannered young lady you've become with the benefits of a private education.

When my dad had proposed Choate to me years before, I just assumed he and my family would see me play girls' hockey in the Northeast during my tenure there and beyond. He had always been my biggest fan. But I was dead wrong. It was emotionally upsetting to know that the one person who got me into this entire circle—Dad—wasn't in Japan to see me in all my glory. At the time I had I suspected that he wasn't going to make it to the Olympics, but I had a reservoir of hope that he'd find his way to Japan and I would see him in the stands cheering me on during the most important games of my life. He had not made it and I had to accept that the older I became, the more he slipped away. I've learned that he couldn't live for me and I couldn't live for him. There was an unspoken agreement that he wouldn't tell me how to live my life, and I wouldn't tell him how to live his. I later decided that I would be happy for him if he was truly happy. He pushed enough to get me interested in the world of hockey but once I graduated from Choate, our relationship took another direction.

▼▼▼

The summer after graduation and after the historic Olympic Games I went home to Michigan. One day early in the summer, I figured it was time to get back on the ice. I headed to the rink in St. Clare Shores for some pick-up games. I had not skated in the past two months, the longest amount of time I had taken off since I started playing at age seven. I made my way to the front counter and handed the older woman five dollars for the drop-in hockey round.

"I'm sorry, drop-in hockey is for men only," the woman said.

"Oh. Is it a matter of locker rooms? I can change in the women's restroom. That's no big deal."

"No."

"Do I need to register?"

"Dear, it's a men's-only league."

"Okay, show me this in your rule book."

She unearthed a rink policy book from a drawer, flipped through a few pages—turning back and forth between pages—then stood up, placed the book on the counter, turned the book to face me, and with her wrinkled index finger pointed at the clause. There it was: *Drop-in hockey is for men only.* "What am I, nine years old and getting banned from traveling with the boys' team again?" I thought. The veins in my neck thickened and I shifted my weight. I fumed for a moment over this travesty and then decided to fight for fairness and equality on the ice.

"Could you photocopy this page for me?" I asked her, with a touch of sharpness in my voice.

"Sure."

Still shocked and generally miffed, I asked her for the manager's phone number when she handed me the photocopy. I stormed off to the nearest pay phone, dialed the number, and got the same woman at the front desk again. Thwarted! I quickly hung up and walked back over to the front desk and locked eyes with her.

"As a woman, do you agree with these rules?" I asked.

"I really don't think about it much," she responded.

"Do you think they're fair and equitable?"

We were interrupted by the appearance of the rink employee who drove the Zamboni, the machine that smoothes the ice surface. He walked into the office and started fiddling with papers, but clearly he just wanted to watch me banter with this woman, who wouldn't accept my five dollars. I hated to bring out the personal accolades, but it was time to validate my point.

"Do you realize I just returned from the Winter Olympics, where I won a gold medal for the USA women's ice hockey team?"

They looked at each other and then burst into laughter. They thought I was lying. I guess they were not among the millions of viewers who saw us win months earlier.

With the paper inside my clenched fist, I muttered, "This is blatant gender discrimination" and stormed out of the rink. Furious, I called a former national team player turned lawyer, Maria Dennis, to get her opinion about a possible discrimination lawsuit. She said suing was a possibility, given that this was a publicly funded rink, but for proof it would be best to get them denying me an opportunity to play on tape.

With tenacious follow-through, I contacted Kevin Roseborough, a player from the Old Devils Hockey Team that I skated with in the summer. He was a lead investigative reporter at Fox News. He pitched my story to the Fox producers, and then agreed to see where the story would lead. The next day, they wired me up with a hidden camera buried in a fanny pack. A different woman was working the front counter at the rink, but we had nearly the same exchange. She wouldn't accept my money for the drop-in league. It was for men only. Perfect, I got what I needed. Only this time I didn't storm out of the rink feeling quite as rejected. This was going somewhere. These folks were going to learn a thing or two about gender politics on the eve of the next millennium.

The following day the reporters brought the footage to the city rink and showed it to rink employees. The reporters asked to see the rink rulebook, and started asking questions about discrimination against women. Mysteriously the rulebook was lost and the workers shifted the blame. The Fox network broadcast the story across the nation, and temporarily I became more famous as the hockey player that battled the city rink for gender discrimination than the hockey player who won a gold medal. You never know how victories are going to affect your life.

When I returned to the rink for a third time, the woman reluctantly accepted my five dollars: I had won. This brought to mind Walter Bagehot's saying that "the greatest pleasure in life is doing what people say you cannot do." I suited up and sprang onto the ice for some play. Over an hour or so, I scored six goals against the men, most of whom were relative beginners, and I realized that the lack of competition wasn't really doing anything for me. After my seventh goal, I called it quits and parted ways with the men I had fought to play with.

No matter how far we think we've come with equal rights, this experience made me realize that pockets of backwardness still exist in society. I guess you never expect it to happen to you. After coming from Choate, where the school had taken a day off for me, then greeted me with a celebration assembly, this slap in the face of women stunned me. The only option that occurred to me at the time was to fight it. As is the case with most injustices, the only thing you can do is keep fighting for equality across all planes, whether it's gender, politics, or ideologies.

It's somewhat ironic that a number of years later I actually held my All-American Girls' Hockey School at this very rink, which was the best-equipped facility for my school and also the closest rink to my house in Harper Woods. The woman that was caught on tape still worked there, but this time she and others were more than helpful and courteous to me. I had battled for women in this rink and now little girls were learning how to defend and score.

▼▼▼

At the end of that summer, Mom, Pamela, and I packed our car with my small but worldly personal possessions and left Michigan for Cambridge, Massachusetts. They were driving me to college, where I was set to walk into Harvard Square, find my dormitory, and meet my new roommates. Not two hours outside our home, while driving through Canada, our car lost its muffler. Luckily, Billy was close by, playing for the London Knights of the Ontario Hockey League, so we decided to drop by the rink while the mechanics worked on the car. Oddly enough, we saw Dad there with another woman sitting next to him, whom I thought was a hockey mom until she scurried away at our approach. Nobody said anything and they didn't have to. Though I had hardly seen my father over the course of the last four years, I did know his face, and the look he had given this woman was unmistakable. I would never have thought a smile would have given away a change in his life, one that would lead to the demise of my parents' marriage. It just went against logic. The happiness I saw in him gave his secret away, a secret my mother didn't yet know.

Since the age of nine I had seen fissures in my home life. Growing up, Billy, Pam, and I knew we didn't have a typical home life. Dad wasn't one who returned home from his satisfying job to put down a briefcase in the foyer and gush about the smell of dinner to Mom. There were times when Mom worked during the day and slept at night, and Dad slept away his days and stayed up at night watching television on the couch. Their opposing schedules led to arguments that made me wish I were deaf sometimes. And when he would leave the house, it was to hustle Billy and me to practice at any hour of the day. Our hockey was my dad's passion. His boot camp-like style of behavior over our schedule, diets, and exercise wasn't like anyone else's father we knew. He never allowed us to have friends outside of our hockey friends. For Billy and me, hockey took precedence over everything else.

It just so happened that before we set out on our Boston trip, I had cashed a two-thousand-dollar stipend I had received

from USA Hockey. Since Mom didn't have the money to fix
the car, I paid for the repairs. It seemed almost simultaneously
while we waited for the mechanics to finish that I received a
call from a compliance officer with the NCAA, the organization that oversees college sports. Compliance officers are in
charge of making sure that schools and athletes obey various
rules about recruiting, scholarships, and the like, including the
prohibition against certain types of financial help. The officer
stated that the NCAA regretted to inform me that the stipend
I had received was against regulations and that as a result of
taking it I was no longer eligible to play college hockey. I had
thought that this stipend was allowed, but by cashing it, I instead had seemingly kicked my college dreams away.

All I now heard was *you cannot play hockey for Harvard*.
Mind on overload. This was turning out to be the worst road
trip imaginable. I told the officer that I had talked to Coach
Stone and the appropriate NCAA officers, who told me it was
acceptable to receive the stipend at this particular time. I was
aware of all of the intricacies of when it was acceptable to receive
money while being a student-athlete. For example, as a college-
bound athlete, I couldn't accept a bonus grant from the
Olympic Committee after winning the gold medal because of
NCAA rules. The only things I could accept were the Team
USA clothes and twenty dollars a day for per diem expenses,
such as buying a Gatorade or something after a game. According
to NCAA regulations, I was also ineligible to participate in any
product endorsements, which was why one morning in Nagano
after the win I turned the corner in the Olympic Village to
find the majority of my teammates working with a professional
photographer for a Wheaties box campaign, with me and the

four other college kids excluded completely. I frantically called the Harvard official in charge of compliance issues, trying to hold back the tears. She thought she could resolve the issue, but this potential disaster would plague my mind the entire trip.

Hours behind on our road trip to Cambridge, we crashed at a hotel in Albany for the night. When we pulled into the parking lot, I told Pam to hold onto my Olympic gold medal for safekeeping. Not a moment later, she accidentally dropped the case and the medal went clink, clink, clink on the pavement. I freaked out and yelled at her, "I will take care of the medal!" As we walked into the hotel room, I looked around for a safe place. I put the medal in the drawer next to my bedside table and thought that this was the only material possession in my life that really mattered to me.

The next morning we took off early for Cambridge. A few hours later we were endlessly circling Harvard Square. We passed the same buildings, the same trees, the same signs. I kept looking down at the campus map and looking at the landmarks.

"Where the hell is Canaday A?" I kept repeating to myself. "Apparently they made a mistake in accepting me here. I can't even find my dorm." Mom kept driving as I squinted out the window, with a nice autumn breeze tickling my lips. Finally, I had her slow down and asked a group of students wearing Harvard sweatshirts where the dorm was. One said it was in *Hahvahd Yahd* . . . the accent gave us a chuckle. After finally locating the building, we each took an armload of my stuff and traipsed up four flights of stairs to find my room and meet my new roommates. We had only exchanged e-mails prior to our arrivals and knew very little about one another. There were five of us in a quad setting, meaning someone was going to have to double up. Since I was the last to arrive they had decided that I was the one to have to double up. I immediately debated their decision and asked that we draw straws, purely out of fairness. They agreed. We drew. I still ended up with the double. It was nice we all could act like adults.

I started to place a few of my boxes in the room when one of my new roommates said, "So, let's see that gold medal when you get a chance."

I immediately experienced a mind-body spasm that must have been akin to an epileptic fit. This was followed by an explosion of expletives. Without even responding to my roommate's request, I sprinted down the corridor, leaped down the stairs, and ran to the car, where Mom and Pam were unloading boxes and clothes.

"Get in the car! Get in the freaking car! We're going back to Albany."

They were puzzled and stood still, looking at me with alarm.

"I forgot the medal . . . my God, the medal! Get in the CAR."

I was completely freaking out and had no idea what to do. As we drove away I turned over options in my head. If I called the hotel they might say they found it and it was in good hands. On the other hand a housekeeper might find it, never say a word, and then hawk it instead for thousands of dollars. We couldn't navigate fast enough through the campus and out of town. I was ferociously flipping through my planner to find a person that could help me in Albany. Finally, we stopped at a gas station with a pay phone and I called the father of a former teammate, Jaclyn Kryzak (who later went on to play for Boston

College). Mr Kryzak lived in Albany and readily agreed to try to retrieve the medal. Pam, Mom, and I sat at the gas station. We gave him the number to call us back. It was the longest half hour of my life. We had to guard the phone so that no one would use it. I was a complete mess . . . with my dad, the car breaking down, the NCAA eligibility, moving into Harvard for the first time, and now I'd lost my gold medal!

When Mr. Kryzak arrived at the hotel, he determined that housekeeping had indeed found the medal and turned it in. A few days later he graciously made his way to Cambridge and handed me the medal in person. By then Harvard and the NCAA had worked out the stipend issue and I was once again eligible to play hockey for the Crimson. Crises over.

To this day, I wonder what my freshman-year roommates must have thought of me on that first day. First impressions are everything, right? And here I was a crazy lady who leapt from the room without warning. They could have easily written me off as a loose cannon . . . the one they'd have to watch out for. To their credit, they didn't and we soon bonded over shared interests and concerns.

▼▼▼

As it turned out, my mom was the one we had to watch out for. Soon after I settled into Harvard life, Dad took off to New Orleans to be with his new woman, whom it turned out he had met over the Internet. Pam decided to move back in with Mom, who needed someone around to fill an abruptly empty nest. When children leave, parents have to get used to no more large grocery bills, no more laundry to step over, no more stray hairs to wipe up in the bathroom, no more worrying about curfew, no more loud music, no more borrowing of the car, no more dinners together near the television. But when your children leave and your spouse leaves, then a life you've lived for twenty-some years becomes unrecognizable, no matter how hard or maddening it was before everyone left.

Sometimes being involved in an unhealthy relationship provides more shelter than being alone in an unknown one. In a sense too, Mom was facing her own Harvard experience in life—an intimidating journey that would challenge her as well as expose her insecurities. And for this, I finally realized she was the glue that had always kept our family together. She was the parent I ended up thinking of fondly rather than my dad as I had done while growing up. I had gone from speaking to Dad every day for four years while at Choate to hardly speaking to him. He slipped from me, and I imagined him in a new life down near Bourbon Street, laughing and drinking mint juleps with the new woman who had taken his soul's embers and turned them into a fire.

Part of me was grateful for his happiness. And part of me, for the first time, was homesick. During all the time I had spent away from home, I rarely ever wished to be back with the family. In a sense, going away to school and spending summers attending and working at hockey camps was my method of running away from an increasingly stressful home life. Arguing didn't have to be part of your daily routine—that was another lesson I learned at Choate. But this time while away at Harvard during the first semester, I wanted to return to Michigan to a home with no more tension, but a brittle bit of peace shrouding it.

I found solace instead on the ice. Being on the ice had always provided me with a sense of peace, because it cast familiarity no matter where I was in the world. Ice is ice, though its surface varies from rink to rink. Figure skaters prefer softer ice; speed skaters prefer harder ice. Hockey players like it somewhere in between. At the beginning of the game, the ice is fastest. It's slower after lots of play, when "snow" builds up from the scraping action of blades. Then, anywhere in the world, out comes the Zamboni to resurface the ice and provide a clean slate for starting fresh again. Unfortunately, there's no Zamboni for smoothing out our troubled emotional lives.

I have always felt the most comfortable on the ice. When I am in my gear I feel secure. It is like putting on an armor of self-confidence. It was an armor that I needed during those dark times of transition. My parents' marriage troubles disconcerted me, and while I had never called a particular house "home," the notion of "home" always went back to my family—particularly the way my family was when I was younger, and things were more stable. Few things bring more insecurity and tension than watching your traditional safe havens disrupted by anger, depression, and broken relationships. Couple that with the enormous stress of not only entering college, but starting at a place I was intimidated by, and it's easy to see why I needed ice—my home away from home—as soon as I got to Harvard.

▼▼▼

The Cambridge/Boston area, with its abundance of colleges, seems to have more college students than windows in buildings and homes combined. At Choate I stayed away from an active social life that might have put me in the company of alcohol, smoking, or drugs. Getting kicked out of school for underage hedonism never seemed worth the risk. But at

Harvard, I wanted to participate in dancing and night life—just being one of the ladies in a social situation sounded right at that time of my life. I mean, I had held off on that aspect of socializing and I had paid my dues. I was ready to let go of curfews and collared shirts. Freedom of choice was going to rule my young world—at least until hockey season started. I could stay up late and wear sweatpants to class if I chose to. That alone felt like a good place for empowering personal decisions.

Placing that many young people at the helm of their lives in a cosmopolitan environment invites flirtation to dizzying degrees. After learning that I played hockey, the recurrent, innocuous pick-up line I heard from guys was, "How much can you bench press?" The social scene was the opposite of Choate—it wasn't your talent but your look that intrigued potential partners. Since age 16, I have held onto my sturdy, Italian-blooded frame, which intimidates some people. Standing five feet nine inches and weighing 180 pounds, I thrashed on the ice and grooved in the club. Most guys I met were more interested in skating with me than making out. Fortunately, though, more so than ever before, society respects female athletes' size and power, as we know from such icons as Serena Williams, Jenny Thompson, and Cheryl Haworth. Accepting your body's composition develops self-confidence. The sooner you accept your body's best, healthy self, the better off your mind is to focus on your sport.

I think this is one of the aspects of women's sports that I value the most. Women and girls who play sports are more likely to accept who they are as complete people. They realize that their bodies are just small portions of themselves. This ability to accept your self-image, however imperfect it is in society's eyes, can become the backbone for self-contentment. I find that girls and women in sport can use their bodies as a tool, rather than viewing it as the definition of themselves. So many images say that larger women are less desirable or less worthy than a pint-size woman. I find it funny, for example, that the average woman is a size 12–14, yet media images rarely show anybody bigger than a 4. I have come to my perception of beauty only through sports and what it has given me. Sometimes I wish my hockey butt would look better in a mini skirt, but I realize that the inner beauty of a person is much more attractive than the exterior components.

As an independent first-year student, I felt my body quickly turning to mush. I didn't necessarily gain the dreaded "freshman 15" from the addition of late-night Tommy's pizza slices, a hot chocolate here, and a sandwich there, but I did tone down my training habits compared to when I had been on the Women's National Team. Within my first year of college, I stayed up later, studied harder, and socialized more. Given the caliber of students in my company, my goal going into Harvard was to obtain a 2.0 grade point average, even though I had graduated prep school with B average. I knew I was up against die-hard students with a sense of entitlement to a big piece of career pie in whatever field they decided to pursue. So, I set low academic expectations for myself and quickly followed in that line.

Freshman year I worked at the dormitory front desk from 6:30 A.M. to 12:30 in the afternoon. I largely used this quiet time to study. I remember thinking that span of time would be enough to study for my first introduction to psychology midterm. I failed that test. The professor pulled me aside and stated that if I didn't ace the last exam, I would fail the class.

I started to cry to him, explaining that at Harvard, one F in a class makes you an ineligible athlete; a D places you on probation. I couldn't afford either one on my transcript. So I decided to change my ways and learn how to study. I figured I may not be the most intelligent person in my class, but if I put the time in to learn the material, then I might have a chance at better grades. For the final psychology test, I read the 250-page textbook twice and studied my notes until I had gone beyond memorization and entered the conceptual world of retaining ideas with a critical-thinking mindset. I aced the test and ended up with a C in the class, my lowest letter grade at Harvard.

From there on out, I realized that I had to set higher academic goals. Also, physical conditioning had to be the priority once again. Harvard had given me a chance, and I needed to repay it, if not for the team then for myself.

Deciding on a major, or concentration as they call it at Harvard, was pretty difficult in and of itself. I started taking psychology and anthropology courses in an attempt to get to know the world outside the academic core subjects drilled into my head at prep school. A liberal arts college offered a pool of electives to further shape my brain and philosophy on life. During my anthropology studies I focused on biological anthropology. This was the closest I would get to a science course without having to directly compete with the brains vying for entrance into medical school one day. I realized I didn't have to be Jane Goodall and travel to the African jungles to study how primates adapt to an environment. Harvard was an academic jungle, and I was the primate trying to adjust.

Harvard, intentionally or not, brings out your insecurities. Had I not had a hockey team to fall back on, if I hadn't known a few students, and if I hadn't graduated from prep school, I would not have chosen Harvard. It simply would have been out of my panoramic view. Yet socializing and graduating from Choate allowed me early on to acclimate to the kinds of students that associate with such prestigious institutions. I remember one year some fellow students talking about a family that had just bought an island. These students with posh winter vacation pads and tropical getaways were not necessarily the happiest kids on campus. In fact, I often found that extreme wealth was equated with extreme unhappiness. If I could be happy and come from a working class family, frankly, that was all the empowering I needed to continue on the path in pursuing my passion.

If anything, an elite education gives you the tools—or the opportunities—to transcend social class or at least partake in experiences that many people from my socioeconomic background wouldn't otherwise have had the chance to do. I'm pretty sure, had it not been for hockey and sympathetic school advisors, I wouldn't have visited Finland, Sweden, China, Japan, and Canada by the age of 18 and another dozen countries since then. When you become part of the upper class—even if by proxy—opportunities open up that wouldn't have otherwise been available. While I don't come from an upper-class family, I now have the education of one of its members.

Hockey at Harvard made the transition to college life a little less nerve-racking, since it had always been a safety zone for me. It's not hard to fit into a new environment when you're already part of a group with a common interest—an interest that brought you there in the first place. During my freshman year's fall semester I was still off the ice, because the NCAA season, which ran through March, didn't open until October. Hockey writers had picked Harvard as the preseason favorite to win the national championship. Coach Stone knew that with our talent and experience, including players such as A. J. Mleczko, Tammy Lee Shewchuk, Jen Botterill (an outstanding incoming Canadian national player), Crystal Springer, Julie Rando, Tara Dunn, Sally Maloney, Kim McManama, and Angie Francisco, we had a shot at taking it all the way. From the beginning, even in our off-season conditioning, there was an unspoken pressure to emphasize performance over having fun.

I believe that one of the factors that contributed to the collection of talent on our team, that brought a group of women together with a similar goal in mind for a sport that used to be for men only, was Title IX. Title IX is a federal statute passed back in 1972 that prohibits gender discrimination in educational programs that receive federal funding—which basically means almost all schools. By implementing Title IX, NCAA schools must offer an equal number of athletic scholarships to men and women. Although the law has been controversial, with some college sports officials claiming it has led to unfair cuts in men's athletic programs, I think that it has been a big factor in establishing women's hockey as a major varsity collegiate sport and has helped it grow exponentially.

I am part of the first generation to really feel the benefits of Title IX. If girls are looking to enroll in a sport with the best possible opportunities to land a collegiate scholarship I tell them that golf, crew, and hockey offer the most opportunities per capita, because there are fewer applicants. Softball, basketball, and volleyball have more scholarship spots but an even larger application pool; hence, athletes' chances are not as good at earning a coveted spot there compared to a spot in a lesser-exposed sport.

▼▼▼

My first two years at Harvard were some of the best years of my short life. I was living a dream. I had the opportunity to get the education of a lifetime. I was playing on the top-ranked Harvard hockey team, and I was making some of the best friends of my life. The people at Harvard and the educational opportunities were allowing me to sort out my views of the world. I was suddenly questioning everything. I was not just going with the flow, but rather, I was exploring social boundaries and challenging every opinion possible to better solidify my own views. I loved the debates I used to get into with my friends, staying up late in the dining halls and questioning peoples' positions on topics such as welfare, abortion, gay rights, and the role of church versus state. I took a moral reasoning class that forced me to challenge even my own views. I guess you can say that I thrived in this sort of environment and loved the challenge of debate. My mother always says that I take after her because she loves to debate . . . and talk, for that matter.

I think that because of my first two years in Harvard, I learned how to speak in front of large groups of people, which later helped me to be comfortable talking to media representatives and continues to help me today when I address hockey schools, Boy Scout troops, businesses, or hockey camps. I suddenly began to appreciate learning in and of itself. But, more than learning anything specifically at Harvard, I learned how to think. I learned to challenge everything and to think for myself.

This has carried over into other aspects of my life. I think I have more poise and confidence because of those fundamental years.

But it wasn't all study and debate. The hockey players loved having fun, and even when I got serious about academics, I still got roped into many strange situations. One of my favorite memories of the Harvard hockey team was stealing Coach Katey Stone's license plate, appropriately named for her favorite sport and number: "Pucks 9." One of my teammates, who I won't name for obvious reasons, actually took one of the three plates we "borrowed" and took pictures of themselves next to it in Europe and then mailed them back to her.

I was always among the main pranksters on the team. When I found out that "Mac" was afraid of snakes, I bought a huge, three-foot-long, realistic-looking snake. While she was showering one day and her hair was lathered and her eyes closed, I put the snake on the floor of the shower. The entire team was in on it, and we were all waiting around the shower to see her reaction. She shrieked SO loud, ran out of the shower, crashed into the stick stall, and knocked all of our hockey sticks over. As others caught on, they preceded to put snakes in her gloves and skates, always eliciting a great reaction. That's just the way our team was . . . always looking for fun.

My teammates also pulled pranks on me, of course. Every year we have a secret Santa for two days . . . and secret satan for one day. The first two days are for small gifts, and the third day is for pranks. My freshman year, our trainer Patty Vasiliadis put up signs all over campus headlined "dating service" and with my name, picture (my hockey mug shot from that year), and phone number. I was totally embarrassed. Good one, Patty.

It seemed like we were always up to pranks like that directed at our coaches or even at each other. What made the hockey team doubly fun was consistently winning. In the years before the arrival of recruits like me, Mleczko, and Botterill, the Harvard women's hockey team had struggled just to stay afloat. Two years before we got there, the team posted a 9–17–1 record. They followed it the next year with a 10–18–1 record in a season in which only 12 players were on the team, and injuries threatened to wipe out the team at any point. Elizabeth Ganzenmuller, a senior when I joined the team, said the contrast between those years and the years after the new recruits arrived was "like playing on two different teams. Before you had to make sure that you weren't hurt because there was no one else to play. Now you're fighting for every shift you get."

In 1999, we rolled to a 31–1 record, which included 30 straight victories and a thrilling 6–5 overtime victory against the University of New Hampshire in the American Women's Collegiate Hockey Association national championship (this was before the NCAA established a tournament for the sport). The season remains the greatest any Harvard team has put together, and I enjoyed personal success by being named an All-American and Ivy League Defender of the Year. My early years at Harvard were also spent with great Olympians—Mleczko, Botterill, and Shewchuk. Seeing how well we worked together and how Team USA had elevated my game prepared me for the next phase, a departure from my new life that I had not quite anticipated.

Clockwise from top left. Always ready to take shots at the net, I couldn't wait to try out my new stick at my eighth birthday party—in pink ruffles! Pam (middle) age 6, Billy age 4, and me age 5 have always been close. The Peewee B Pasadena Maple Leafs: 1992–1993 state champs (Billy is the goalie, Scott Plumer is on the far right). Two of my teammates and me at an awards banquet in 1991 (as usual in my youth, I am the tallest one among the boys).

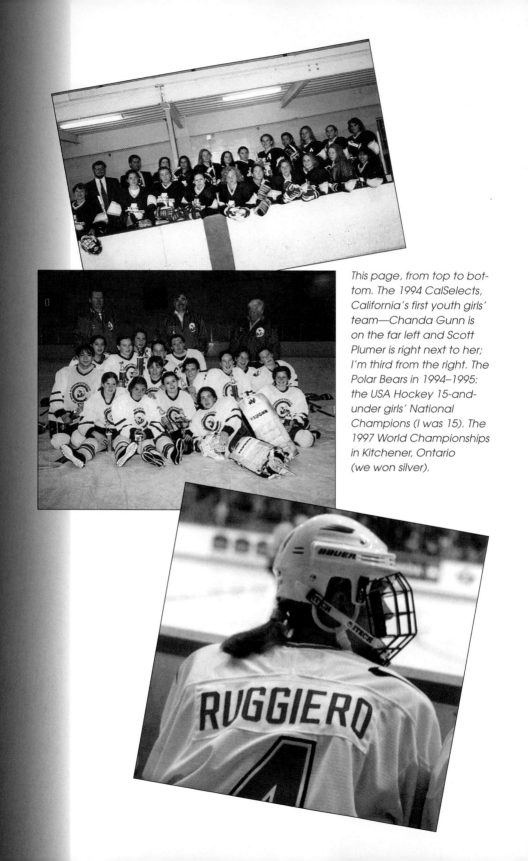

This page, from top to bottom. The 1994 CalSelects, California's first youth girls' team—Chanda Gunn is on the far left and Scott Plumer is right next to her; I'm third from the right. The Polar Bears in 1994–1995: the USA Hockey 15-and-under girls' National Champions (I was 15). The 1997 World Championships in Kitchener, Ontario (we won silver).

Harvard Athletic Communications

Robert E. Klein

*This page, from top to bottom. The Choate Rosemary Hall 1998
Track and Field Team, where I threw discus, javelin, and shot to
enhance my off-season training, captured the New England
Championship. My 1999 Harvard teammates and I gather just
after the National Championship (I wore #3 that year) game
and out and about on campus in Cambridge. Team captains
Lauren McAuliffe and I with Coach Katey Stone flaunt Boston's
coveted Beanpot Trophy in 2004.*

B. Bennett Getty Images Sport

This page, from top to bottom. The 1998 National Olympic Team poses in our opening ceremony attire in Nagano, Japan—I am on the far left in front. Just after the final buzzer at our gold medal win over rival Team Canada at the 1998 Winter Olympics, we gathered for a team photo on the ice.a fan gave me a huge American flag—I took a victory lap while Canada looked on. The official 2002 Olympic Team photo.

This page, from top to bottom. At the 2002 Winter Olympics in Salt Lake City, I clowned around for the camera while waiting for the opening ceremonies to begin. I treasure the memory of this meaningful walk into the ceremonies with the flag recovered from the World Trade Center on September 11, 2001. Following our loss to Canada, I hug teammate Krissy Wendell while we receive our silver medals.

US Olympic Committee

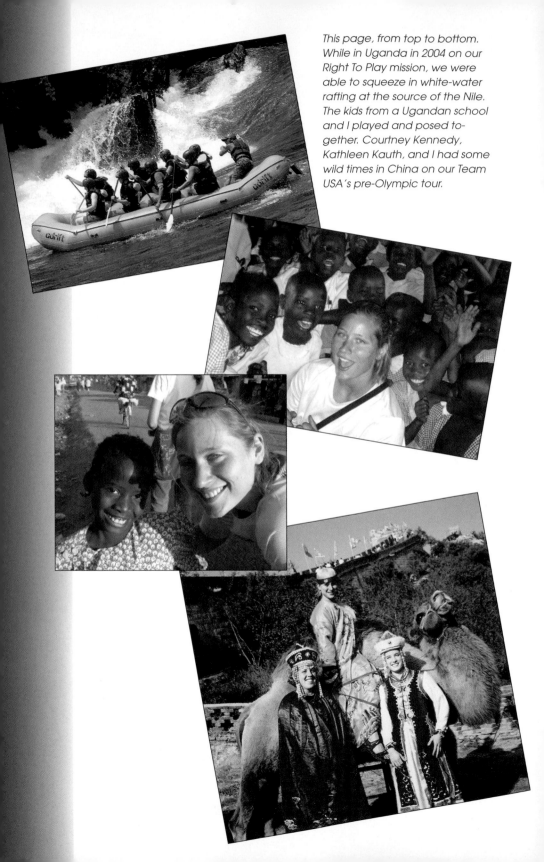

This page, from top to bottom. While in Uganda in 2004 on our Right To Play mission, we were able to squeeze in white-water rafting at the source of the Nile. The kids from a Ugandan school and I played and posed together. Courtney Kennedy, Kathleen Kauth, and I had some wild times in China on our Team USA's pre-Olympic tour.

This page from top to bottom. The IIHF 2005 Women's World Champions pose with our medals, and Cammi Granato, Jenny Potter, and I raise the trophy after the win. Billy and I before our Tulsa Oilers game where we were teammates again. Mom joined Billy and me for a photo before the Tulsa game—she came to cheer us on!

Getty Images

Getty Images

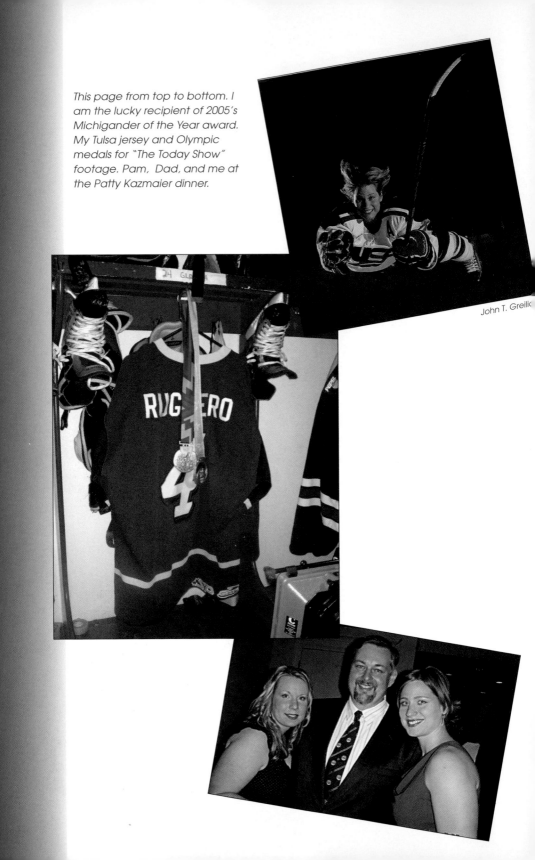

This page from top to bottom. I am the lucky recipient of 2005's Michigander of the Year award. My Tulsa jersey and Olympic medals for "The Today Show" footage. Pam, Dad, and me at the Patty Kazmaier dinner.

John T. Greilic

CHAPTER *6*

String of Silver

I'm showing off my silver medal after the final game of the 2002 Winter Olympics in Salt Lake City.

Top, I'm making a pass at
the 2002 Olympics. Left,
practicing with the
Women's National Team
in 2001.

Neil Negsted

*I*n 2000, the year before the NCAA officially announced that women's ice hockey was to be a varsity sport, I contemplated leaving Harvard for two years to train full-time with the U.S. Women's National Team. Before the 1998 Olympics, the National Team had played in various tournaments around the world, and we had been through a series of cuts to get down to the final team. But there had been off-season times, breaks when we trained on our own, stayed with our families, tended to school or whatever else we had going on.

Our success in those Olympics caught the eyes of the U.S. Olympic Committee and of USA Hockey. They wanted to see women's hockey mature as a sport in the United States, and hoped for another gold medal in the 2002 Winter Games, due to be held in Salt Lake City. The two organizations invested heavily in the women's ice hockey program, and so they decided to have the team live, train, and play together from late 2000 until the time of the Games in February 2002. In addition to that, much as it did before 1998, the team would tour the United States and the world. A Visa-sponsored "Skate to Salt Lake Tour" would not only prime the team for the Olympics but also provide widespread exposure for women's hockey. Not only would this be a great opportunity to prepare for the Olympics, I would be part of something that could help pioneer the sport.

Committing to the Olympics might sound like a simple decision, but women's hockey was changing on the college level as well. In 2001 the NCAA was scheduled to run its first national championship tournament for women's ice hockey.

I had a chance to help my team, and the teammates I cared deeply about and had played with for two years, win this historic championship. During that junior year I was also going to be one of the team captains. Taking a year off from college hockey would be difficult physically—my body will not remain young forever and I did not want to have any regrets.

I have to admit that I didn't do a lot of rational thinking about hockey during the decision-making process that summer before my junior year. I was on the brink of burnout, a stage almost every athlete (and everyone, for that matter) reaches when he or she has done something for so long. So when my college friend Laela Sturdy invited me to accompany her on a road trip that summer, I accepted. We were set to travel around the Pacific Northwest to rewrite a *Let's Go* travel book. I needed time away from the ice, from red brick buildings, cobblestone streets, and hockey gear. Going on a road trip was a somewhat unusual lifestyle choice for the average Harvard student, many of whom had prestigious summer internships in consulting and investment banking, ready to set them up for post-graduation experience and jobs. Instead, I opted for spending time in hostels and tents while listening to the Dave Matthews Band in a rental car as we cruised the mountains and valleys of Oregon and Washington.

▼▼▼

For the entire six-week trip I didn't pick up a hockey stick or lace on my skates. Sitting in a car for nearly six weeks made my body soft but happy. For the time being I didn't care to complete any workout routine other than a day-hike here and there. I'm a firm believer in taking time off every couple of years when the tinge of burnout peeks its ugly head into your life. That summer job—really, more of a vacation—was about me taking the time to discover what my next step would be: return to Harvard for my junior year and the chance to win the first-ever NCAA trophy, or postpone college to train full-time with the Women's National Team for the 2002 Olympics. Both options offered various chances to excel, strengthen my life, and help my sport, but I kept coming back to the personal question: *Which decision would leave me with the fewest regrets?*

As we weaved our way up and over the Cascade Mountains, I received a call from my mother. The spotty cell phone coverage cut her off every few seconds but she was perfectly clear when I heard, "We're getting a divorce." Over the past two years my parents had tried working out their differences. Dad had left twice and had come back twice. This time it was for good. He was leaving us for a happier life he had finally found with another woman. Hockey no longer gave him the satisfaction and glimmer of hope that it once had. His kids were grown up, out of the house, and fulfilling their own destinies. Now it was time for him to fulfill his, I guess. Mom was always a preacher of happiness: "Do what makes you happy." Life is too short to stay in an unhappy situation for too long.

That summer on the road, I called Coach Stone and Coach Smith three times, each time with a different decision about whether to return to Harvard or to play with the Olympic team. I was at a crossroads within my own relationship to hockey teams. *Which one would I desert first?* I thought. *Who am I going to let down more?* As we entered the mountainous terrain of northern Washington, thick, gray clouds seemed to camouflage not only the horizon but my future. I wondered if both coaches had started to lose respect for me because I kept waffling on this tough decision.

Looking at Mount St. Helens, the site where, in 1980, the year of my birth, a volcanic eruption sent a mushroom-shaped cloud blasting into the sky and devastated more than 200 square miles of terrain, prompted a final decision. Like eruptions, decisions simmer and shake until they burst forth. I realized that I would have only a handful of moments to shine. When you boil down life, it really is a series of shining moments. Everything else, the in-between moments, are when you do most of your living—the kind you don't think too much about.

When it came down to my young life, I determined that what I wanted most was another chance to win a gold medal and train as a professional athlete with the rest of the Women's National Team. Harvard and the NCAA would always be there, though the teammates I came in with would not—they would graduate and be gone before I returned. It was an early divorce from them, but for me I knew the rest of my life could wait if I needed it to. The Olympics come around only every four years. Now was my chance to be part of a larger history once more, because I wasn't sure if I'd ever have the opportunity again. More than anything I didn't want to return to college and regret not having tried to train full-time with the rest of the Olympians. I did not want to leave any doubt that I did all that I could for my team and for myself. I was the last player to commit to Team USA and the first one to cry when I told my Harvard teammates I was taking a temporary hiatus.

▼▼▼

At the end of that summer, I made my way through another set of mountains on the opposite side of the country. This time I was alone. The sheer cliffs and the river running along the two-lane highway made me smile at my hyperactive geographic meandering as I drove over windy roads carved into the Adirondack Mountains in upstate New York, on the way to the Olympic training camp in Lake Placid.

I must have been born with a gene for nomadic pleasures. Being tied down to any one place for an extended period of time hadn't been part of my life since the age of 14. I have called "home" to almost a dozen houses with my parents in California and later in Michigan, and an equal number of places throughout my dorm life. Increasingly I wanted to live a life light on possessions and big on experiences. Some classmates at Harvard consider postponing a college degree by two years as losing time toward bankrolling some serious cash. Money mattered very little to me. Women's hockey is a feast-or-famine kind of lifestyle. No player (either then or today) pulls in a hefty salary just for becoming a professional female hockey player. The recently established National Women's Hockey League (NWHL) offers the closest thing to a professional league. The competition is fierce, but the payroll is not: you do not get paid to play, but your expenses are mostly covered by hockey sponsors.

Nor have the days yet come when players can earn six-figure endorsement deals. The hockey equipment company Bauer and the iconic athletic company Nike are among the main sponsors of women's ice hockey right now, and deserve our thanks for supporting the sport at a time when its popularity has yet to reach its potential. We're still trying to have scores—and our stories—reach the sports pages in national newspapers on a regular basis. You have to love something a lot to accept reaping few financial rewards from it. We do it for the love of the game and for the passion that inspires us every day. I think this is one of the main reasons that our fans love our brand of hockey. Women's hockey at all levels is played out of pure love. The camaraderie of the team is what I will miss the most when I finally hang up my skates, not the fact that, for the most part, I have to scrape by to play.

Spending a year at Lake Placid seemed like a great opportunity on many levels, but being away from the social hub of college had its pitfalls. I wouldn't say training full-time was depressing, but the experience lent itself to a drastic culture shock after the cosmopolitan campus life I had come to adore. I missed biking across the Charles River to the rink, spending time in my dorm, staying up late watching movies with friends. I missed our Harvard pregame locker room ritual of belting out "We're Not Gonna Take It" by Twisted Sister. I missed singing, with junior Sally Maloney, one of her hilarious, made-up songs that she used to entertain the Harvard hockey team. I missed my Dunkin' Donuts coffee in the morning. I missed such Harvard hockey lingo as ATM (Ate Too Much), KB (Kissing Bandit), HP (High-profile Player), and JS and HKPK (sorry, but my teammates would slaughter me if I made public these last two acronyms) that we used in order to keep jokes from Coach Stone. I missed the luxury of going online to order a Slurpee and movie from Kozmo.com, a small Internet-based service that would hand-deliver convenience store items to your dorm room. (Kozmo, like a number of other dot.coms, would bite the dust before I got back to Harvard.) I guess it was better for my Olympic aspirations in the end to get away from all of these distractions, but at age 21 I longed for a little more adventure to life than the weekly movie, soft drinks from Stewart's, and a dash through the quarter-mile-long main street of Lake Placid.

Being stowed away in the mountains with other athletes is nothing like a spa experience. Forget fluffy down comforters and personalized cotton robes. You won't find individually wrapped gourmet chocolates on your pillow at night. We lived in dormitories that had a daily maid service for linens and towels, but that was the extent of posh catering to athletes' whims. There were few frills other than putting in hard work and vying for a shared dream. But the U.S. Olympic Training Center did have its perks, including everything you needed to train like a champion. I should also mention free rehab for an injured athlete, although nobody ever wanted to be in that position.

When other winter Olympians were not at the training facility at the same time as we were, the cafeteria team offered cook-to-order meals. Salmon, steak, wraps, you name it and they graciously obliged our taste buds when we weren't in the mood for the salad bar or pasta bar. Beginning at the age of 14, when I had started my nomadic search for hockey opportunities in the world, I had become a connoisseur of cafeteria cuisine. In any given year I might have had a handful of homemade meals. Otherwise, I organized, stacked, and filled a colored cafeteria tray—often so well I could do it with my eyes closed.

Oddly enough, cafeterias and dormitories became "home" to me over all these years. I hardly know what it means to have private, personal space. When you're part of a team, the idea is to break down your space and share your life with others in the name of bonding. During the training year, we all agreed to have an open-door policy. Whenever you were in the dorm, you left your bedroom door open. We didn't want anyone feeling isolated or alone. Each player left behind her family and normal way of life to pursue a sports dream. On any given day, we wanted to elicit opportunities for camaraderie.

When we were not training we looked to fill our time, almost like retired people. I had every intention of learning to play the guitar—I had the instrument and the books—before I realized that it was harder than I had thought, since I could not read sheet music. Instead, I opted for the potting wheel with about six of my teammates, or watched Lifetime with Laurie Baker or Sara DeCosta, or read *The Poisonwood Bible* or *The Power of One* alone in my room. The pottery at least allowed for a few personal touches in an otherwise bland room. Without the rigor of Harvard academics, and with so much time devoted just to playing hockey, I feared that my mind would go to mush. I guess I agree with the philosophy of Leonardo da Vinci: "Iron rusts from disuse, stagnant water loses its purity, and in cold weather becomes frozen: even so does inaction sap the vigors of the mind." So, I spent downtime with my nose in a book.

Tuesday was our only day off. Not much happening on a Monday night so I was usually in bed at a decent hour. I tried to pack in a traditional weekend's worth of routines into one day. First there was the selfish pleasure of sleeping in until mid-morning and lounging around the cafeteria and drinking more coffee than normal. Then a group of us walked about five minutes away to downtown Lake Placid to shop at the Gap

Outlet, browse around the other local shops, or see a movie at the small theater. While living at the training facility, Team USA gave each of us a monthly stipend for personal bills and needs. With no car payment or tuition, I bought myself more clothes during that period than probably at any other point in my life.

The brunt of the team's relationship came through the shared experience of the body aches we endured while training. At 6:30 A.M. we were required to be dressed and ready to run outside with the team. My roommate, Krissy Wendell, and I, neither of us morning people, created an exact science of setting the alarm clock with four minutes to roll out of bed, get dressed, tie the shoes, and meet the team on time. Rain or snow didn't matter—we ran regardless. When it was dark outside, coach told us to wear light-colored clothes so cars and people could see us. One day we came dressed in white workout clothing to find that we blended in with the snow that had fallen during the night.

After the run, we ate breakfast and then headed to the rink for a two-hour practice. We followed that with lunch and then two hours in the afternoon of strength and conditioning training and sometimes a stationary bike workout of 45 minutes. Our coach recorded our heart rates on these tests and we had to keep them above 90 percent of capacity for five-minute intervals, followed by three minutes of rest. Every so often we would also meditate with our sports psychologist, Peter Haberl.

This routine shaped our lives six days a week. Training became a mental game for me. I realized that it required you to dig deeper inside your psyche to acknowledge the pain that was speaking very loudly in your head, or better yet, in your ear—I sometimes imagined a little woman waving her arms while jumping up and down on my shoulder and telling me to *stop the madness*. Focusing on breathing techniques that Peter taught us diminished the pain during our resistance training or bike workouts. I stayed focused on the exercise and eventually I made it through another repetition, another minute, and saw the end in sight. As Aristotle once said, "We are what we repeatedly do. Excellence then, is not an act, but a habit." We had to make every aspect of our game a habit, to create this excellence on the ice.

▼▼▼

Overall, I'd say the hardest part of the whole experience was actually the mental toughness of doing the same thing, day in and day out—something I learned again, three years later, at my first "real job." To perform your best, no matter how mundane or repetitive the task, is the core of excellence. Instead of just going through the motions to get my workout or job done, I always try to do each task to the utmost of my ability. In this sense, I am not just passing the time or doing only what is required of me. Instead, I am actually *developing* and growing as an athlete and person. It's not just a cliché to talk about putting 100 percent into every act you do, be it sleep (personally I love a completely dark room), work, or play (my teammates from the first years of Harvard can confirm that I did this rather well). Coach Stone at Harvard used to always say that when you cross the Charles River to skate at Bright Hockey Center, leave your academic and personal lives behind and fully dedicate yourself to the art of becoming a better hockey player. I try to live this way in every aspect of my life. I try to leave behind my worries and problems, whatever I've confronted during the day, and focus on the immediate task in front of me.

Of course, mental preparation takes time, and at Lake Placid it required the help of the team's sports psychologist. It takes effort and practice, just like developing strong legs and a carved core. You have to realize as an athlete that, in addition to talent, longevity is one of your greatest assets. For example, the regular NHL season runs 82 games; men's and women's college hockey teams play 30 to 40 games in a season; and the pre-Olympic tour has a 35-game schedule that merges into the Olympic schedule of up to 5 games. Even though the NHL has more games, those players do not work out off of the ice in-season as much as college athletes and Olympians do, because of the sheer volume of games they play each season. Nevertheless, athletes must work on their on- and off-ice conditioning in order to sustain strength, speed, and longevity during a season. It not only aids in the prevention of injuries, it also allows equally talented teams the chance to play into overtime (if needed) and battle it out until the bitter end.

Often after numerous shifts in a hockey game, when two teams match each other on talent, one will prevail based on better conditioning. Lactic acid, the chemical that causes you to feel fatigue in your legs after sprinting, is bound to build up in your legs, but preparation and conditioning can mean the difference. I would have this confirmed most dramatically three years later, when I competed in the NCAA tournament and averaged more than 44 minutes of ice time (out of a possible 60 in a regulation game) per game. My coach depended on me so much that I knew I had to be in top condition to play this many minutes. (I do, however, have to thank my parents for blessing me with such great genes. Both my brother and I have been tested and we possess lungs 150 percent larger than average. That means that we can get more oxygen into our blood, thereby slowing the effects of lactic acid.)

Health and wellness mean not only eating a balanced diet of protein, vegetables, fruits, and carbohydrates, but also staying drug-free. The U.S. Anti-Doping Agency (USADA) tests and monitors America's Olympic athletes to make sure that they remain free of performance-enhancing drugs. As an Olympic athlete in training you are required to tell the USADA where you will be every day of the year so that they can find you on any given day and, if they want, administer a drug test. The consequences are serious if athletes don't measure up to their side of the agreement. For example, if USADA reps show up to where you're supposed to be and you're not there, it counts as an "X" against you. If you receive three of these "X's," a two-year suspension follows. A positive drug test is an automatic suspension.

The testing procedure is the same for everyone. One day after hockey practice at Harvard, a few USADA employees showed up to conduct an unannounced drug test. Once they approached you, they monitored your every move. They watched you finish your workout, watched you shower, and then watched your urine stream enter a cup. They asked you a series of questions about your diet and any medications you recently took (over-the-counter, supplements, and prescription drugs). Generally, if I get sick I try not to take any medication, and just let my body fight off the illness naturally. That way I don't have to worry about anything on a random drug test possibly showing up. It would be my worst nightmare to unknowingly take a banned substance because me AND my entire team would be disqualified during competition if I tested positive, so I steer clear of almost everything but clean protein and a multivitamin.

Most athletes test negative, particularly when it comes to a more skill-based sport like hockey as opposed to an athletic-based sport like sprinting. In hockey if you don't know how to skate and handle a stick, you're not going to get very far no matter how bulked up you are. Yet in track, athletes have pushed their bodies to extremes with the help of performance-enhancement drugs. It doesn't happen very often, but it is a concern that the USADA keeps in check to uphold the integrity of competition within each sport. I am all for it.

▼▼▼

After a year of training, we took a few months off. At the Women's World Championships in April 2001, we had won a silver medal, losing to Canada 3–2 in overtime, despite the year of training as a team. We had expected to win the gold after everything that we had put into the previous year, but somehow Canada managed to beat us again. I was disappointed and frustrated that even after taking the extra year to train with the team, we could not beat Canada when it counted the most. It was a real letdown for the team, but we were inspired to work even harder in the off-season to prepare for the largest competition of all the following year, the Salt Lake City Winter Olympics.

During our time off, I moved to Boston to train with Harvard teammates Kat Sweet, Tracy Caitlin, Jamie Hagerman, and Kalen Ingram. In the time I was not taking my course on

American foreign policy at Harvard, I was sweating away in the humid heat of Massachusetts. Our trainer ran us into the ground that summer, forcing us to do a two-and-a-half hour workout four times a week. We warmed up for 15 minutes, did 10 minutes of abs and core, 10 minutes of plyometrics, 15 minutes of foot-speed drills using cones and hurdles, and then a 45-minute lift, followed by a 30-minute bike or running workout. It was painful, especially when the weather was hot and we had to do resistance sprints using parachutes or bungee cords. I think it was a little easier for me when I put the Olympic rings in the back of my mind—I then had the ability to dig deeper. Somehow those five rings have always conjured up emotions and energy reserves that I have down deep.

After my summer training, I headed to Lake Placid once again. We had a two-week tryout composed mostly of games. Evaluators sit high above in the rafters and talk about you, out of earshot. There are usually two teams that are vying for the 25 roster spots that will go on tour. The whole process of making the team is very similar to what was depicted in the movie *Miracle*.

I was selected once again to represent the United States on the "Visa Skate to Salt Lake Tour." The Women's National Team traveled from Montreal, to Vancouver, to Boston, to California that year. The team was supposed to travel to Finland for the annual Four Nations Cup, but the September 11 terrorist attacks occurred and that trip was canceled. Tours like these not only provide us competition but also promote the sport of ice hockey. In order for a sport to grow, there needs to be a following. The only way for young girls and fans to follow a sport, however, is through the media, where coverage is spotty at best, even in pre-Olympic years. Fans have to rely on a few web sites, such as USCHO.com and USAHockey.com, that closely follow hockey.

Traveling from coast to coast and even abroad to bring women's ice hockey into the limelight, if only for a few months, is something that the members of Team USA feel lucky and privileged to do, as the torchbearers for future generations of young and aspiring Olympians. I for one can tell you that there is no better feeling than meeting a young girl who says that she wants to be just like you when she grows up. It is great to know that she can have the opportunity to play at one of 70-plus NCAA institutions that offer women's hockey, and there's the growing possibility that many can go further than that. Having a positive role model is a powerful thing for girls, especially when they can see a girl doing something as well as the boys.

Thus, we pack our USA duffle bags, hockey bags, sticks, and backpack for seven months straight to promote the game and help it grow. In 2001–2002 alone, we played 31 games in the United States, Canada, and China. Anticipation about the Olympic Games grew with the success of the tour—we won all 31 games, including 23 against international opponents and 8 against college teams, and we outscored our opponents 252–27. Most significantly, we beat Team Canada eight times without a single defeat across the continent. We rounded out our training in Steamboat Springs, Colorado, again using this city's particularly high altitude to train for the 2002 Games. After a week of feeling light-headed from the elevation, we packed our bags and bused to Salt Lake City to start it all. Gold was on our minds.

▼▼▼

The scene at the 2002 Olympics was a stark contrast to that of 1998. In many ways, the world had changed—in some good ways, but in more dark ways—in those four years, and with it, I had changed, as had the hockey team. For me, the newness of my first Olympic Games was gone, replaced by the pressure and anticipation of the USOC and USA Hockey, which had invested much more heavily in the team. In 1998, our victory meant that a lot of sponsorship money was available to start professional leagues and grow the sport in innovative ways, but the organized bodies of women's hockey at the time hadn't been prepared to respond. Now they were, and they wanted a gold medal to seal the deal.

Women's hockey started the Olympics front and center, as Cammi Granato climbed the steps at Rice-Eccles Olympic Stadium carrying the Olympic torch toward the Cauldron at the Opening Ceremony. It was a moment that all North American women's players—Canadian and American alike—appreciated for its significance.

Entering the Games, I reviewed what I had been through in four years since the last Olympics. I had seen my parents' marriage finally collapse. I had gone through a period of burnout, then the wrenching decision to join the team and put off my Harvard teammates. September 11 had also cast its shadow over everything. The world gathered for the Games, and the media spotlight was as bright as ever, but many questioned whether the Games could be played, even should be played, with the security threats that hung over the event. The security precautions were tighter than ever, and the extra tension was everywhere.

More than that, the tragedy of September 11 reached into my own life and that of Team USA. Kathleen Kauth, who later made the 2005 Women's National Team, had been one of the last girls cut from the 2002 National Team, and she was one of my good friends. As a team, we had suffered with her when her father, Don Kauth, died in the collapse of the second of the World Trade Center buildings. At the 2002 Olympic opening ceremonies, we had the usual parade of nations scheduled. In addition, the USOC chose eight U.S. athletes, one from each major winter sport, to join New York City police officers and firefighters in carrying the tattered flag from the World Trade Center onto the field. I was one of those eight, selected to walk with the flag, in remembrance of Kathleen's father. I remember talking with Curt Kellinger, one of the Port Authority police officers, before carrying the flag onto the field, and we had an instant connection. He immediately became one of my heroes because of his actions on that day. We've remained good friends ever since and have even gone skydiving together.

When we emerged from the darkness onto the field, the light shone on us and the world seemed to fall silent. We marched forward toward the end of the stadium and then presented the flag before President George W. Bush, who saluted us. A tenor sang the national anthem as the crowd watched in silence. All I could think about was Kath and her father and my friend Sally Maloney's brother Teddy, who was also lost in the attacks. It was one of the most moving experiences of my life, and when I joined my team to enter as part of the parade of nations, I was subdued and choked up—a feeling completely different from what I had experienced in 1998.

Overall, when I compare these two Olympic experiences, I realize how much they reflect the changing shapes of our lives. For many of us, our young lives are full of promise, hope, and soaring achievements that suggest the potential we have inside, the vitality and brilliance of life. As we grow older, we see and experience life's darkness—dreams that don't become reality, deaths of friends and family members, monotony in daily routines, the jarring disconnect between our expectations and reality when we fail. For me, all of those seasons of life were crammed into the three weeks that comprised the 1998 and 2002 Winter Olympics.

The Salt Lake City Olympics weren't without their fun moments and times of personal satisfaction. While the security presence was especially tight, the Olympic Village and the Games were still great places to be. I remember dancing with Coolio on stage and giving him a kiss on my way off stage. I remember meeting Nelly Furtado, who had recently lit up the charts with "I'm Like a Bird." I also deeply appreciated seeing my college friends there to support me: Sally Maloney, Angie Francisco, Laela Sturdy, Tanya Hvizdak, and Maria Palomar-Nebot. Best of all was seeing my mom, sister, and brother. My brother was playing goalie for the Moncton Wildcats in the Quebec Major Junior Hockey League at the time, but they allowed him to miss a game to see me play. He traveled over 24 hours to get to the gold medal game, a journey that required a total of eight planes, just to see me. And in the end, I delighted my sister by giving her my medal ceremony jacket (which a collector had offered to buy for $1,000) for her birthday.

▼▼▼

Despite these good things, the 2002 Games were a personal and athletic disappointment. On paper, it appears that we steamrolled through the Olympic tournament before the gold medal game—we outscored our opponents 31–1. But that figure doesn't reflect the adversity we faced as a team and I faced individually. Just before our opening game against Germany, I caught the worst flu of my life—think mono in its first week times ten. I played the game without complaint, but in the shower, I cried my eyes out from the pain. Though the bug persisted for several days, I played because I couldn't bear the thought of not playing after all we had been through together as a team.

Unfortunately, the bug swept through more than half the team throughout the tournament days, and before the gold medal game against Canada, two of our best players, Jenny Potter and Katie King, were tied to IVs to try to overcome the effects of the late-arriving bug.

The gold medal game was a renewal of our rivalry with Canada, and with our 8–0 record against them over the previous year, we had every edge you could want. In the first two minutes, we saw that edge evaporate as Caroline Ouellette of Canada scored the first goal and they seized the psychological advantage. Worse still, Canada got hit with penalty after penalty, yet we didn't capitalize during the first period. Those consecutive power plays actually wore out our best players. At last, in the second period, Katie King tied the game, but just minutes later, Hayley Wickenheiser took the lead back for Canada with a goal that made it 2–1. With one second left in the second period, Jayna Hefford gave Canada its third goal.

Karyn Bye got us our final goal with four minutes left in the final period, and we fought desperately in front of a wildly cheering home crowd to tie the game. But Kim St-Pierre, Canada's goalie, played a brilliant game in which she fended off 25 of our shots. And just like that, our two-year quest for gold—a personal high we all wanted and a potential push for American women's hockey—was over.

Immediately after the game was one of those moments where you cannot wait to see your loved ones. My mom, sister, brother, and friends were all there to support me, even though we had lost that day. They were sad only because I was. Fans, family, and friends didn't seem to mind that we placed second, because they were able to see Team USA in action. Unless you've put aside two years of your life and forced yourself to focus myopically on one goal, one game, then winning the silver might seem like an accomplishment. The entire team agreed to leave behind their normal lives for two years to work for this one moment to shine, and we did not succeed.

In the aftermath, I replayed the championship game in my head while riding the elevator, washing my hair, walking, holding conversations. Failure filled my mind. We had failed to capitalize on chances the Canadian team had given us. Whatever could go wrong did. Choppy play took over our finesse-and-flow style of play. On our home turf we did not defend the inaugural gold we had so proudly won in 1998.

I have to give Canada credit. They played phenomenally that game and never let up on us. Coach Smith always says that if you were playing golf and you were tied going into the last putt, you would hope that the other player would bury his or her shot because it would force you to play at your best. You never want to win as an athlete, or in anything for that matter, if your competition is not playing at their very best. Canada showed up that day and played a great game. They killed power play after power play. They deserved to win. Call our play poor mental strength under pressure on the home ice. Call it physical misfortune from teammates being sick with the flu. Somehow, we had choked under the pressure; we weren't ready for the pressure of playing in front of our home crowd where almost everyone was chanting "USA!" We had focused on the end goal (winning) as opposed to the experience and process. Instead of letting the game come to us, we played on our heels and never applied the pressure or had the same confidence that we had in our undefeated pre-Olympic tour. No matter how many excuses we might try to muster, we did not gel as a team that night. Losing is part of sports. Losing is part of life. That still didn't stop our tears from flowing.

We had won a silver medal but it was an enormous failure in our own minds and those of many who had invested so heavily in us. In women's hockey, there's a tremendous amount of pressure to perform each time on the ice. In our sport, since its inception as an IIHF-recognized event in 1990, the final has always been U.S. versus Canada. In essence, you could win every game in a season, but the only one that matters is the final, whether at the World Championships or the Olympics. We play to win the final game of our season and the media and rest of the world remembers only one winner. In a sports world where there is enough room only for those who win, "The Tonight Show," *Time*, *Sports Illustrated*, and news programs were not knocking on our doors. (Hometown cities did, however, organize many great receptions for various women players. For example, Harper Woods, Michigan, did a great job of honoring me with the fire department and local girls' teams showing up for cake in the City Hall.)

But it is the final game that counts the most. Thus, there is always the end goal of winning in our heads and at times this goal compromises the need for us to focus on the process. In order to reach "the zone," that elusive personal space where time slows down and you seem to perform almost effortlessly, you need to focus on the day-to-day aspects of the game that you can control, like making the perfect pass or shot. You also want to relish every moment of playing, because a player's days are limited. I know that I will look back and remember the smell of the rink, the joy of dancing to Enrique Iglesias's "Escape" in the locker room, the tap of a teammate on my shin pads when I need a little help, the feeling of making a clean and crisp pass to Krissy Wendell who is cherry-picking (cheating up the ice) down the middle lane, or the pain of performing bike sprints. As William Feather once said, "Plenty of people miss their share of happiness, not because they never found it, but because they didn't stop to enjoy it."

I think that we focused too much in 2002 on the end goal and not enough on enjoying the little things in hockey and life that make it all worth it. To elicit a passion is to find joy in these little things and I fault myself for not absorbing the chance of a lifetime in 2002. In the end, I was given the Directorate Award for being the Top Defenseman at the 2002 Games, but that personal achievement was hollow compared with not winning the gold.

▼▼▼

It's funny how your memory of something wonderful in your life, such as the 1998 Games for me, stays crystal clear, whereas my memory of the disappointing 2002 Games doesn't compare. My most vivid memory of the Olympic final game was one of me hitting the goalpost on a power play shot in the second period—a shot that was an inch away from tying the game. I thought about my missed opportunity time and time again during the months after the Olympics.

I had plenty of time to do this when I decided to get away from it all after the Olympics. I needed the break and I needed to reevaluate my life. I find that the intervals in between the actions in your life are the periods in which you learn the most.

What I did was travel around Europe with Kathleen Kauth on a Eurail pass for two months. I did not have any rent to pay, nor even a car payment, and had saved a little money in my checking account for a trip. Kathleen was the perfect travel companion and we used to talk for hours about various social issues, politics, or just the beautiful landscapes of Europe. We even visited ex-teammate Annamarie Holmes and a few of our other friends on the trip. I quickly fell out of a routine somewhere near Greenwich Mean Time. Egg whites—a high-protein, low-fat staple of training—were out of my life. Fruit became an option. Croissants and cappuccinos were the staple of a late morning breakfast. Wherever we stayed—in hostels or hotels—I lived out of a backpack and very little in my head. Instead of replaying the loss over and over again, I stayed *in the moment* of the day I was witnessing. With such amazing landscapes, works of art, and people all around you, it was hard not to. Without consciously searching for the answer to why we lost that last game, my lack of routine sort of sparked it serendipitously: I needed to focus less on the outcome and more on the moment. It sounded so simple to say, but living it and believing in it became two different paths. My new mission was to try to get my mind and body to follow that philosophy.

We spent eight weeks traveling, from the Red Light district in Amsterdam, to the famous operas in Vienna, to the Guinness factory of Dublin, to the beautiful bridges of Prague and the picturesque beaches of Mykonos Island. The time I spent sipping Lilly espressos in Italy and beyond was time I needed to deal with one of the most devastating losses of my life. The question of "had I done enough?" rang over and over again. It's as if I woke up one morning and wondered what all the hard work was for. Was it worth it when you come in second? *Second. Second. Second.* I think I hate losing more than I love winning. I am naturally competitive at anything . . . even a friendly game of cards with my sister. I couldn't get being second out of my head, considering that we went into the gold medal game undefeated. To this day, years later, it still pains me when someone talks about that game and asks how we could lose after being 8–0 versus Canada that year. I usually get defensive because although it was just a game that they watched on TV and perhaps bet five bucks on, it was my life.

The searching for reasons why we did not capture the gold resonated in my head for the first month or so, but then I began to better understand my journey. I had to miss the U.S. Olympic Team's visit to the White House that year because of my journey, but I knew it was the right decision. I returned from that trip with a good feeling. My team had done everything possible, I realized, and the chips just did not fall in place. I had postponed Harvard for two years, left my friends and family for my surrogate sisters in Lake Placid, and trained harder than ever in search of a second gold medal. Instead of walking away with regret, I walked away with a silver medal and a newfound determination to fall in love with my sport once more. "There is only one thing more painful than learning from experience," Archibald McLeish said, "and that is not learning from experience." I promised myself to do anything possible to help our team next time around, including recognizing the unbelievable opportunity we have. But arriving at this conclusion wasn't easy. I had to go deep inside myself to reach it, and in many ways, I'm still searching for some answers that elude me.

▼▼▼

With a new focus on enjoying the journey and savoring moments, I returned to Harvard to play two more seasons of college hockey and complete four semesters worth of requirements. I am lucky that the NCAA recognizes the efforts of NCAA athletes by allowing them four years of eligibility over six years. Thus, I had a clean slate. Two more years with the Crimson as one of the team captains and two more years to relish the college experience.

What happened over the next 24 months was another lesson in maturity. When I returned to Harvard, everything was different—much as I expected it to be. The teammates I had played with were all graduated, except the kids who had been freshmen when I was a sophomore. Now they were seniors, and I was a junior. Socially, I knew it would be a challenge since I was older than everyone, and since I would be playing with a group of people who had taken control of the Harvard team.

You would expect there to be some difficulties, at least early on. But I gelled with the team right away. I sensed that they respected me for the time I had left to join them and were proud of me for the medal I had helped win. As well, we had a common, singular focus—we badly wanted the NCAA national championship. That common goal and our mutual respect soon led to good times and fast friendships. I loved to dance in the locker room with Ali Crum, Lauren McAuliffe ("Cully"), and Kat Sweet to "Sandstorm," the latest techno tune, or shoot the breeze with my roommate, team goalie, and overall intellectual Jess Ruddock. My teammates became like sisters and gave me a new family away from home.

Off the ice, I suddenly realized that I needed to focus more on my studies and take advantage of the forty-thousand-dollar education that I was offered. I decided to move away from the regular Harvard social scene and devote myself to studies that I truly enjoyed—I switched my major from biological anthropology to government in order to pursue my newfound passion in international relations. I raised my standards in the classroom and set my sights on straight A's. I also decided to volunteer at the local elementary school and became the co-chair of the Harvard-Radcliffe Foundation for Women's Athletics on campus. This organization was devoted to getting more women involved in sports and to having a louder voice in the athletic community at Harvard. Harvard, with more Division 1 sports (41) offered than any school in the county, was the perfect place for the foundation to offer a way for half of the athletic community to stay involved and connected. I also joined the Women's Leadership Project and attended as many lectures from visiting professors as I could. Instead of the fraternity surfing and partying life I exposed myself to in my first years, I opted for quiet time in my dorm studying. I became quite the geek if I do say so myself. I was suddenly not embarrassed to announce that I was studying on the bus . . . a feat that is hard to do on a hockey team even at Harvard. I engaged myself in things outside the rink that made me think and grow as a person.

That year, our strong mix of seniors and experience propelled us to a number two ranking near the end of the regular season. We stormed through the NCAA tournament by beating the University of Minnesota in the semifinal and we were slated to play Minnesota-Duluth in the final. But against Minnesota-Duluth, we soon found ourselves in a dogfight like none we had had that year. The game was heated and the score went back and forth. We were down 2–0 after the first but came storming back to set a record for quickest goals and tie the score within the first minute of the second. A few minutes later we scored to go up 3–2, but they quickly caught up to us, making it 3–3. The third period was scoreless and there were many opportunities for each team, but our goalies kept us in it. The game ended up going into overtime, but there was no score after the first 20-minute overtime period. Halfway through the second OT though, they scored on a wrist shot from the top of the circle. The game could have gone either way and the crowd of over 5,000 was cheering louder than any smaller capacity rink I can remember.

The game is now considered a classic of NCAA women's hockey. And while I take pleasure in having participated in it, I was heartbroken when I watched the puck float past Jess Ruddock, who was screened on the shot. I was a first-team

All-America selection for the third time, and one of three finalists for the Patty Kazmaier Trophy. (This award, like the Heisman Trophy in football or the Hobey Baker in men's hockey, is given to the best all-around college player each year, one who displays outstanding individual and team skills, sportsmanship, performance in the clutch, and a love of the game. It is named after a former Princeton standout whose father actually won the Heisman Trophy during his playing days in college football.) I had also led the nation's defense-men in scoring for the third season, yet that all paled in comparison to this loss. Like the Olympics, I succeeded personally, but the team failure pained me more than the personal success could compensate. I wanted to win so badly that year with my team but again the chips did not fall our way.

I comforted myself until the next season, knowing that I still had another shot at an NCAA title. We started that season rated number five in the nation, mainly because we had lost the previous year's Kazmaier winner, Jen Botterill, but we had some great underclassmen stepping up to fill in other holes. Despite the ups and downs that year, we won the Ivy League title, the four-school Boston-area Beanpot Trophy for the sixth straight year, and the Eastern Collegiate Athletic Conference title (by beating Brown in overtime). Then we rolled through the NCAA tournament, beating St. Lawrence to make it to the final game.

That year, in addition to being named the ECAC and Ivy Player of the Year, I was awarded the Kazmaier Trophy. The night before the national championship, I attended the award banquet. The evening, a very emotional one for me, combined my hockey world with my family world for the first time since my parents' divorce. Both parents and my father's new wife attended that night, and while I had to strategically place my mom and dad apart, I was happy to have them both there. My brother and sister also attended, making it the first time in years that the whole family was together. When I was presented the Kazmaier award, I went to the podium, looked out over the audience, and paused. It is rare in life that you get a podium to tell the important people in your life how much they mean to you. I took full advantage by thanking my teammates, coaches, and former coaches, and then thanking each family member individually. Despite the general physical absence of my family from my life the last few years, their presence that night meant everything to me, and I felt truly proud not only to receive the award, but to be a Ruggiero.

▼▼▼

The perfect ending to that story would be Harvard winning the national championship the next day. But the Minnesota Golden Gophers had a first line made up of my Team USA teammates Krissy Wendell, Natalie Darwitz, and Kelly Stephens. For the first two periods, we hung with them, kept the score tied, even dominated at times. Kat Sweet and Nicole Corriero scored for us, but then that powerful first line overwhelmed us with four goals in the third period. Our season, and my Harvard career, was over.

My co-captain Cully and I had to face the media after the game, and both of us struggled to fight back tears. I hated the second-place finish, and I hurt inside knowing that I would hang up the Crimson jersey forever. Somehow, it felt like another dream had been suddenly and sharply crushed.

Today, I'm able to look at the photo of Cully and me accepting the runner-up trophy and laugh. Our faces are sullen, our hair was absolutely everywhere. Cully even refused to take off her helmet until the league commissioner made her. Neither of us cared what we looked like—we hurt too much to focus on what we'd look like in a picture.

My final two years at Harvard were full of other personal accomplishments that I remain proud of to this day. In 2003, I won the USA Hockey/Chevrolet Women's Hockey Player of the Year award, now named the Bob Allen Award, and I made history in 2004 by becoming the only player to win it twice. Two newspapers in 2003 named me the best defenseman in the world, and *ESPN* rated me as one of the 16 best female athletes in the world in 2004. I was also ranked as the #1 female hockey player in the world by *The Hockey News* in 2003.

Perhaps, though, the personal awards I'm most pleased with are ones that combined my academic discipline with my love of hockey. For the 2003–2004 school year, the NCAA named me one of the Top VIII recipients. These eight scholar-athletes are selected from all NCAA sports and divisions for academic achievement, social engagement, and athletic excellence. I'm also very proud of being named a CoSIDA (College Sports Information Directors of America) First Team Academic All-American, honoring 816 student-athletes annually who have succeeded at the highest level on the playing field and in the classroom. I tried so hard and in my senior year brought my grades up, proudly graduating *cum laude* from Harvard, the very place that had initially intimidated me into striving for a mere 2.0 grade-point average.

Personal achievements have come naturally as part of my ongoing hockey pursuits. But since the 2002 Olympics, team achievements have grown ever more difficult to reach. My college career was over with another pair of runner-up trophies to display on the mantel back home in Michigan. After my most recent season, playing for the Montreal Axion of the NWHL, the nascent professional league for women, my team lost in yet another championship game. Eight in a row—one Olympic gold medal game, two NCAA finals, four World Championship games, and an NWHL final game! I had lost eight major championships in a row, watching the other team throw their gloves into the air in jubilation at the final buzzer.

It's fair to ask what the point of continuing was. If I've already won Olympic gold and a collegiate national championship, if I've already won most of the significant individual awards a woman hockey player can achieve, why not move on to something else, especially when team achievements have become so challenging? In part, the answer is the challenge. I want to help my team, whatever that team is, get back to the top, to feel again that connection that comes from winning the whole thing with a group of people you've grown so close to. I guess people can say that I have been blessed to be on a team that had made it to that many finals in a row, but I can reply that it makes it that much harder to lose and to lose with such great groups of women, such an amazing collection of friends. I love the time I get to spend with them, so it makes it even harder to lose with them.

Beyond that, this long period of second place has refined me, taught me the value of pushing through pain and striving to excel even when no one is watching and the results aren't adding up. I've learned something about the process of *becoming*—that is, becoming a better, more well-rounded person. I've broadened my circle of friends, and I've become more patient with people and with the need to win. I've accepted that I can't always make everything come out right, that some dreams won't be fulfilled, that in some ways, it's not the achievement of a dream but rather the pursuit of it that makes us the best we can possibly be. I've learned that many people are watching me and my sport, even though that number may pale in comparison to the number watching other athletes (hopefully that will change soon). I have a responsibility to those people and to the thousands of little girls who are waiting to have an avenue paved for them. And I have a responsibility to others in the world who have never heard of hockey or seen a rink or a puck. My connection to organizations, media, and sponsors gives me a forum to help people just joining hockey, as well as people in poverty-stricken countries where sports can be a point of connection and belonging.

CHAPTER *7*

Dry Land

Laela Sturdy, Alexis Sturdy and I kneel in front of the students at an elementary school in Uganda.

Curt Kellinger and I do a tandem skydive in 2002.

*A*s I wrapped up my college career, I hit one of those strange spots a female hockey player, and most women athletes, encounter at some point—I had almost nowhere to play and no team to train with. I had reached the ceiling of women's athletic progression. Because the only women's professional ice hockey league, the NWHL, is in Canada and because league rules limit how many foreign players can join a team, there were few options to take my game to the next level. For women in most sports, once they leave college, their careers are over, unless they can win a coveted—and highly competitive—spot on the national team. And even then, playing on the national team only postpones the inevitable.

I knew I wanted to prepare for the 2006 Olympics, but other than that, I was unsure what to do with my life. What would life be like after hockey? I often pondered this question as I finished up my last semester of college. It seemed that I needed to prepare for a life beyond hockey, even if I was able to combine hockey with other events of my post-graduation life.

In addition to that dilemma, my outlook had changed significantly from when I first arrived at Harvard. Graduation gave me a marker, a clear point in time to trace the trajectory of my own growth. I had come to Harvard literally at the top of the world—an Olympic gold medalist with a great prep school education who was entering one of the nation's oldest and finest institutions of higher education. These experiences had been made available to me despite a youth characterized by frequent moves and economic ups and downs—periods of no money, Christmases without presents, school years without new clothes. Because of my abilities on the ice, I had the where-withal to obtain an education that could open doors for me throughout the world, and I felt like I could do anything in the world I set my mind to.

But even in such a situation, my Harvard and 2002 Olympic years had taught me how easy it is to fall, how closely failure stalks all of us, how uncertain sports could be, and how athletics could not remain my only plan. The 2002 Olympics had sobered me to the reality that even the best-laid plans, the best training, and the best institutions could not guarantee present or future success. The subsequent runner-up finishes in tournaments also helped me realize that there were aspects of life, aspects of success and failure, that were beyond my own control. I could not guarantee a gold medal or a national championship or a world championship just by being the best defenseman possible. On the other hand, I learned a liberating truth—that whatever team success or failure I might be part of, I could always guarantee that I had given my all, done all I could to help my fellow teammates be the best they could be, no matter what the adversity. This understanding helped clarify many things for me.

I also learned that my success didn't shield me from the emotional struggles that life brings. My parents' marriage had come apart, just as my athletic achievements seemingly reached a pinnacle. No amount of success or good behavior inside or outside of my family could change that fact. And while it wasn't necessarily my failure, I had a responsibility to connect with and to assist my family. Whether I approved or disapproved of anyone's actions, I needed to do my best to sustain the relationship, and to build on the common ground, I had with each parent.

While I had learned that great preparation couldn't always prevent failure, I had come to appreciate how much preparation molded and shaped who I was becoming. And of course I knew that my chances of success were better if I was adequately prepared for the challenges ahead. I had thus discovered that just walking out of Harvard with a degree wouldn't guarantee success in any venue—athletic or otherwise. But if used wisely, a degree from such an institution could greatly benefit me personally. Also, as I would with any hockey team I played on or with any member of my family, I could reach out and do my best with a broad spectrum of people beyond my own experience. This realization helped focus my studies while in school, and it helped broaden my perspective: I needed to do more for others than I had, and I needed to do things to prepare myself for a life beyond hockey. But how?

Over the years, hockey has afforded me opportunities to travel to distant countries, meet all kinds of people, and experience various lifestyles. The more I saw, the more I decided I wanted to give back rather than just keep taking in experiences. At some point I started to feel spoiled and selfish for culling all these experiences, with little reciprocation to the larger world community. I was an international relations major, after all, and studied all of the wars and conflicts that occur to this day in the world. In the back of my mind, I wanted to find an opportunity to give back to the less fortunate because I had been blessed with so much over the years. While I do believe hockey offers lessons in self-confidence, teamwork, competition, and discipline, I know that hockey might offer more to the world, even if most of these children had no idea what my sport was. To that point in my life, I just had not seen it yet.

My first inclination was to look beyond myself to a Toronto-based humanitarian organization, Right To Play (RTP), that I was already familiar with. Right To Play uses sports and play programs to benefit some of the world's most disadvantaged children, from Azerbaijan to Zambia. I found out about RTP from Nikki Stone, a fellow athlete-ambassador and an Olympic gold medalist in the skiing aerials event. This was during the summer of 2000, at a time when I was unable to devote much time to the organization. I did donate some autographed items and attend a fundraising function here and there, but I wanted to do more. Working with the United Nations, Red Cross, and other agencies, RTP recruits Olympic athletes and volunteers to spend time with children in developing countries and poverty-stricken areas of the world. RTP groups are trained in activities that help promote, for example, AIDS awareness through play and games.

Studying consumed much of my life during my final spring at Harvard, but I also found time to get involved with the organization. My friend Laela Sturdy and her younger sister Alexis developed a proposal for a trip to Uganda, which we pitched to Right To Play, and the organization approved it. I felt like I could help in this area and was appointed the fundraiser for this trip. My efforts were somewhat modest—I basically wrote a letter and set up an e-mail address, advocating for the cause and describing the itinerary of the trip. I sent the message to all of my friends, associates, and contacts—anybody that I thought would be willing to help. I was surprised at the overwhelming support, and within three months of receiving clearance and support from Right To Play, the $17,000 needed for the trip was in the bank.

When an athlete tries to do some good in this world, people seem to respond, perhaps only because it seems to be above and beyond what is expected of an athlete. It always amazes me when athletes or movie stars receive more support for their particular causes than the average Joe, just because of their status. It seems to me that athletes and celebrities have a responsibility, then, to be involved in good causes and to choose carefully what to support and how to do it. I applaud celebrities, like Bono of U2, who use their status to raise funds for worthwhile causes. I guess that was, in part, what I was trying to do. It's the sort of thing that, to me, should be the rule among those in the public eye, rather than the exception. As Gandhi once said, "Be the change you wish to see in this world."

▼▼▼

Once our funding was secure, we got a series of shots, purchased our tickets, read up on the history of Uganda, and packed our bags for what became one of the most amazing adventures of my life. Forty-eight hours after I had left my home in Michigan, we landed in Kampala, the capital of Uganda, a sprawling city with a strange contrast of modern commerce, convenience, and poverty.

We were greeted by one of the local volunteers, Peter B., who helped us get acquainted with Kampala and the work that RTP was currently doing in Uganda. The stark differences between the life I was used to and life in Africa were seen immediately. Being tall and white got us looks from close up and afar. Strangers muttered the word *muzungu* (white person) on a regular basis as we passed them in the airport or on the street.

It's great to learn the native words, even if they were at our expense. Peter helped us settle into our apartment in Kampala and exchange currency. We visited an Internet café—the most reliable way to send messages to parents or loved ones—and stopped by a grocery store, which was very modern and stocked with almost anything you would find in an American market—ah, the global commodification of brand-name products. I was halfway around the world and still had a sense of home because of its offered goods. We purchased lots of water and a few other items for the summer. We went home in a *mutatu* (a taxi bus). You pay a small fee to travel around the city, which ends up feeling like a heinous amusement park ride as the driver whips around corners and slams on squeaky brakes to avoid taking out pedestrians. One of our first mutatu trips resulted in cries and screams from the scared passengers.

After some rest and time for adjustment, it was time to start work. Peter told us about Sport Health and SportWorks—projects that RTP had set up in the region. He took us to a Sport Health project in one of Kampala's slum areas, where Alice, another local volunteer, was playing games such as ABCD. In this game, A stands for abstinence. (In Uganda, English is the official national language and is taught in grade schools.) The children run to one corner and shake their heads from side to side screaming, "ABSTAIN! ABSTAIN" (from unprotected sex). B—be faithful—prompts the kids to run to a second corner and grab another child by the arm and yell "BE FAITHFUL!" C, for condom, has the children again running to a different corner saying, "USE A CONDOM." And finally D means "DEFECTIVE!" Here the kids crossed their wrists, implying the defective use of needles or other sharp objects.

This game gave the children a means to learn how to prevent HIV/AIDS through sport and play.

We also played a game in which the kids hid a marker behind their backs and the other team had to guess who was holding the marker. This game showed the kids that you couldn't tell who has AIDS by perception alone. I wondered who in the room might have already been infected, which child or children might have lives and family relationships cut short by disease and death. I realized almost immediately that the world's devastations not only encroach on youth far earlier than children should have to bear them, they can affect these young people just as deeply as adults.

After Kampala, one of our first Right To Play destinations was the rural area near Sironko, not far from the border with Kenya. Along the way, we stopped at a roadside stand where we bought fresh-cooked corn on the cob for about 100 shillings, or about 8 cents. As I worked my way around the cob, feeling the warm kernels lodge between my teeth and wishing I had some dental floss, I caught sight of Mt. Elgon, the massive volcanic mountain that dominates the landscape in the area.

After 45 minutes traveling on a red dirt path, we reached Sironko. When we stepped out of the van, children serenaded us with a mixture of native songs and cries of "muzungu, muzungu!" The children—some with giant smiles, others covering their mouths with their hands—were in awe of such white skin in their equatorial land. We held out our hands and connected briefly in the universal game of "gimme five." Some of the kids wore raggedy clothing that looked like hand-me-downs from generations ago. Other kids wore matching baggy uniforms, which were intended to last through their entire schooling. When I looked at their faces, I again wondered which of these children were already suffering from AIDS. Health education was only just beginning to spread to such rural areas. Inside, my heart broke for those whose lives would be so devastated.

We traveled from the rural east to Kibale in the west, with many stops along the way. In most areas, the reactions were similar to those in Sironko. At each school we tried to help teach them Right To Play games, like Dodge HIV, a dodgeball game that symbolized how to dodge HIV, as well as the HIV awareness game of ABCD. Even in desperately impoverished areas, children screamed with joy and laughed as they played with the red soccer balls given to the communities, and on the tire swings and the playgrounds volunteers built for them. Children are children no matter what part of the world you visit.

On occasion, our experience wasn't quite like this. In these instances, the students ignored the games and instead mobbed us as we brought out our digital cameras. Most of these kids had never before seen their own faces in pictures, so the instant screen on the camera became the looking glass of their choice.

In an environment where everything was dirty, the food was bland—bananas, rice, and beans were the main fare, and some rural homes were 10-feet-square mud huts with metal rooftops, I realized that sexual encounters must be the one pleasure this population could afford, although one that could represent a great danger. An act so fundamental to life was killing so many—the ultimate double-edged sword.

Following our visit to Kibale, we spent a week in Mbarara, where we participated in RTP's SportWorks program in the Orichinga and Nakivale refugee camps. The camps are made up of people who fled Rwanda during the genocidal slaughter that took place there in the 1990s, resulting in more than a million dead. I am sure that most of the Western world still does not realize the extent of the atrocities committed, during a time when much of the international community refused to intervene and try to protect this population. The refugees' existence is meager—mud huts with no running water, poor sanitation, and rampant disease. But it's an upgrade from the horrors they fled. They had stories that made me want to cry through the nights—of family members and friends hacked to death with machetes in front of their eyes, of villages turning on long-time residents and murdering them, of narrow escapes on foot across the border to flee the slaughter. I felt powerless in the face of the horrors they endured.

I was speechless hearing their stories, and I think of them to this day. It seemed that playground equipment and soccer balls were such small things to offer, but the smiles on the children's faces when we were pumping up new soccer balls for them and distributing the balls to the local volunteers to look after told otherwise. Their eyes just lit up when they saw us pulling a bright red ball from the bag and handing it over to them. Christmas in the middle of the July! And somehow, that reminded me of the beauty of childhood, the universality of it, the hope and innocence that seem naturally embedded into it, no matter what part of the world children come from. In many ways, offering the tools to play was as life-giving as bringing water, medicine, or food. Giving them the means to play brought these children what all children around the world should have: a space for imagination, a place to leave behind the individual horrors or challenges that they have encountered and let imagination and fun reign. I knew my mission as a sports ambassador was worthwhile, if the only thing it did was create this small island of imagination and play for them.

What stays with me the most from our travels is something that was nearly universal: singing. Almost without exception, these children and their choirs would break into a full song and dance and leave us delighted. I am still singing their playful and joyful songs in my heads, especially our theme song, "Right to Play, Right to Play, Look after yourself, look after one another," and I wonder often how they have the strength to sing so joyfully when they have encountered such adversity. The only answer, I suppose, is that they choose it as an alternative—they sing to make connections with others, to open their hearts and experience joy, to look for brighter days ahead.

▼▼▼

As you can imagine, despite my efforts to give back rather than take in, I was learning and soaking up as much of the experience as possible. And I confess, we took breaks from our volunteer work to take in the majesty of the country. The connection to wildlife in Africa is essential to most people's way of life—few people are shielded from animals and the forces of nature in the ways that North American city dwellers are.

While there, we went on a walking safari, where we saw spectacular wildlife such as rhinos, zebras, warthogs, impalas, buffalo, crocodiles, eagles, and hippos. We also visited a chimpanzee sanctuary on an island, where over 50 chimps had been captured from the wild and saved from poachers or the nearby deforestation. We also white-water rafted at the source of the Nile River, encountering grade-5 (extremely fast-moving) rapids throughout the trip. I'm proud to say our raft turned over only three times.

Beyond that we hiked the mountains and were three of six people lucky enough one day to gain a permit to go mountain gorilla tracking. This was the most spectacular, and haunting, animal that we saw while we were there. The mountain gorilla epitomizes much of the difficult relationship between humanity and wildlife in Africa. One population of gorillas lives in a mountainous region on the border of Uganda, Rwanda, and the Democratic Republic of Congo (DRC), and the other lives in the Bwindi Impenetrable Forest on the border of Uganda and the DRC. There are only about 650 of these animals left in the world. They live in groups of as few as 12 and as many as 30, with a silverback (an older male whose hair on his back has turned silver) as the leader.

Tragically, they are most threatened by humanity—they have no other enemies. Rebels fighting in Rwanda or living in Congo and raiding Rwanda have been known to kill the animals for bush meat, and some have been wounded or killed in the crossfire of rebel battles. In addition, logging companies have increasingly encroached on these forest regions, and in doing so, they have opened the areas up to greater numbers of poachers. Poachers kill the gorillas for the meat, which they then sell to the workers of the logging companies. Poachers are difficult to track and prosecute, and the number of kills is hard to know because the poachers often complete the kill, sell the meat, and see it eaten within a day.

On our trip to the Bwindi forest, we left early in the morning and traveled with a tracker and armed guards (who ward off dangerous wildlife as well as hostile people). The hike and search were strenuous—the forest isn't called "Impenetrable" for nothing. It's dense, with large trees and thousands of varieties of plants, all of which retain lots of moisture from frequent rains. The gorillas take time to track because they move daily looking for food. It took us several hours, and when I wondered if we'd ever see them, we were suddenly upon them in thick brush.

We saw 11 of them, with the silverback larger and more imposing than the others. They seemed comfortable with us being there—they have grown very accustomed to human visitors. We weren't allowed to touch them or to get within 15 feet of them, because they are susceptible to human diseases (hundreds have been wiped out by the Ebola virus, for example).

But seeing them like this and realizing how comfortable they were with us helped me feel a connection to them and to the diverse, beautiful forest they inhabited. They were tall and powerful-looking, yet I realized how fragile they were and how, like children and other innocents, they suffered first and most heavily when humans harmed each other and exploited their natural resources.

▼▼▼

Those four weeks in Uganda passed too quickly, and the amount I had taken in and learned seemed to dwarf what I had given. When I returned to America, I realized hockey was a form of pleasure and pain for me. I was lucky enough to go back to a clean apartment where I could leave my dirty rucksack at the door and take a long, hot shower—an action that few ever got to experience in Uganda. I realized that I took for granted the simple amenities of daily life in our rich society, from a functioning phone system to healthy food to paved roads. Our sense of normality couldn't have been further apart. And it was that realization, that full experience I had in Africa, that created a deeper commitment in me, not just as an athlete, but simply as a human being.

I think that all professional athletes, and people for that matter, should be socially aware—not just of the difficulties abroad, but of the tragedies that haunt our own cities and towns. Whatever our station in life, we all affect each other, and our position in this world is largely arbitrarily chosen. I was lucky enough to be born and raised in the great U.S.A. and therefore have been given the opportunity to succeed and live a peaceful life. I realize that I have been lucky to receive expensive schooling from both Choate and Harvard, and earned degrees that allow me tremendous choice and freedom. My education and hockey have enabled me to do so much, and I feel the obligation to give back. I realize that I can just live my own life, but I would rather share it with others and, hopefully, inspire a few young individuals to do the same. When I work with little girls and young women, I tell them that it is within their reach to do great things. I tell them that it is possible to do anything that they put their minds to. It is possible to get good grades, go to college, and even win a gold medal. I think that I have always had hope in my life and I want to instill confidence in the future into every child's mind.

I realize, as well, that my time in the limelight is fleeting, that it will be only a matter of a decade before I'm largely forgotten, except perhaps by a small crowd of hockey aficionados and the handful who have memories of seeing me play in the Olympics. But the loss of celebrity does not end my obligation.

I hope some day to have children of my own. I hope to be in their schools, helping them and their classmates. I know that my sister, who recently gained her teaching certificate, has already enlisted me to speak in her high school science classes for next year. I have done this for years and it always gives me the chance to reach the nonhockey-playing kids. I hope to work in my community, both within hockey and outside of it. There's an endless amount of work to be done, and I'm not sure that whatever I can offer will add up to much, but I know it will mean something to the few whose lives I touch.

▼▼▼

Returning home from Africa also meant it was time to finalize the transition from school life to "normal life." To me, my life as a traveling athlete was normal, whereas for many others working a steady job with two weeks vacation was a normal life. After the Africa trip, I was bracing myself to take on a new version of normality. School and travel were behind me. Life in the world of the day-to-day economy awaited me. And I had no idea what I was really in for.

I couldn't afford to live in Boston without working. My rent and car payment alone warranted a job. Then there were the expenses of auto insurance, utility payments, groceries, etc. The financial demands of independent living were rather eye-opening, unlike my bohemian days as a student-athlete.

Ideally, I could combine my passions for travel, hockey, and international affairs into some kind of career choice. But the answer wasn't overwhelmingly clear. Other than teaching and directing hockey camps every summer since age 15, writing for a travel guide, working as a skate guard at a local rink (where I also had the luxury of cleaning toilets), a few jobs like stacking thousands of chairs and cleaning hundreds of dorms for Harvard graduation, and traveling the nation and world as a hockey player, my résumé for the corporate world looked pretty dismal. What employer wanted to hire a hockey star with a Harvard degree and no work experience? I was pretty sure I could make coffee at an office, but that wasn't exactly what I had in mind. I knew how to win Olympic medals and give everything to the task at hand, but I wasn't sure I would know how to sit at a desk for eight hours a day.

Like any smart kid, I started with my first line of defense: my mother. Mom had been working in residential real estate since we moved to Michigan and her business at RE/MAX had begun to flourish. With her stories of working in real estate in my mind, and my general interest in this career, I decided to try to find something in that industry around the Boston area. It seemed like a plausible step forward into adulthood. When nearly three-quarters of your life has been lived one way, however, starting fresh isn't something that happens overnight, or even over a summer. Change is also about loss. Many parts of me questioned if hockey had merely extended a youthful obsession or if I could sustain a life with it after I was no longer insulated by an educational institution's team. And here I was, now in my mid-twenties, trying to navigate an entirely new adult life but seemingly lost in a foggy sea. Sometimes the hardest thing in life is not knowing—even more so than having high expectations for yourself.

During the spring and summer of 2004, I started the interview process with companies in Boston. Even before I started working a network of friends and associates for contacts, I contemplated what I was looking for in an employer. Flexibility was high on the list. I still couldn't let go of the dream of being a professional hockey player after graduation. I wanted to start a career in the business world as well as train for the 2006 Olympic team. In order to do this I needed at least six weeks of vacation, to be taken in chunks of time here and there for training, traveling, and tournaments. And then I needed an extended leave of absence the following summer so that I could train full-time with the Women's Olympic Team. From my nonathlete friends, I knew that this much time off in your first job out of college—particularly when you have little corporate experience—wasn't going to be an easy sell. Most people don't get that kind of time off unless they've earned it over the course of years of steady employment with a single company. Two of my national teammates, Tricia Dunn and Katie King, had worked at Home Depot in its Olympic Job Opportunities Program, which allows Olympic athletes in training a flexible part-time work schedule, with full-time pay and benefits. I knew this was an opportunity I could fall back on. I also contemplated and interviewed for a marketing job at Dunkin' Donuts, since I loved their coffee so much.

Life after Harvard often guarantees stellar connections in just about any industry. Not only does the degree cost a bundle but it also offers an extensive network of possibilities. I found my first job through my ex-Harvard teammate and friend at Harvard, Cory Bennett, and her father, Bill. He put me in touch with long-time hockey fan and commercial real estate mogul Tom Hynes, president of the Meredith & Grew real estate firm in Boston. I hit it off with Tom as well as vice president Kristin Blount, one of Boston's "40 under 40" young professionals. I found out that Tom and his family had even hosted NHL star Joe Thornton of the Boston Bruins for a time at their home, after Joe arrived in Boston still a teen, fresh from the junior ranks. Tom's daughter played hockey in college and his son also played hockey as well as football at MIT. The company seemed exactly the right fit, as it would offer me a chance to start out as an associate, learn the commercial real estate business, and earn a decent income for the first time in my life. I arranged to have a formal interview after I returned home from my trip to Africa. The delayed interview already convinced me they were willing to be flexible as I pursued my passion.

▼▼▼

I wish I could say that this seemingly ideal situation worked out perfectly. My transition to the corporate world was as disorienting as my first time on ice, and took much longer to become satisfying. I was used to a regimented diet, vigorous physical activity every day, and mentally challenging myself in the classroom and in my studies. About a month into my job at Meredith & Grew, I knew why office people became "working stiffs." On the days that I was not helping out Kristin, ascending the high-rises of Boston and showing the open floor space to clients, my job basically involved sitting at a computer all day, analyzing reports, and preparing presentations. Sometimes after hours of sitting I'd get up with squeaky joints and tight hip flexors. My first office job also contributed to my first experience of upper back spasms. The mouse cupped in my right hand for nearly eight hours a day caused a huge knot in my upper right shoulder, which then began to spasm. My body just wasn't used to sustaining one position for such a long period of time. Out of nearly 18 years of life on the ice and bone crushing hits, it was a desk job that served up a typical hockey "injury."

Early on, my dietary regimen nearly fell apart, as well. Although I used to drink the occasional cup of coffee before exams or hockey games, the working world offered me frequent refills and a new addition: the daily donuts, muffins, and baked goods that our secretary, Susan, would advertise over the intercom. I learned quickly that I needed to pack a lunch and a healthy snack or two, or I would be growing my waistline much faster than my Olympic muscles.

Beyond even these small adjustments, there was a different sort of pressure to perform. In just my first month on the job I had to fill in for a senior co-worker at a real estate convention in Toronto. I had already bought my first set of six suits to fit in, realizing that I had little in my closet that could be mistaken for dressing for corporate success. The convention itself went fine, and I gave my all to representing the company well, but it was disorienting, and I frequently found myself listening more than talking.

Even then, I could look at these experiences with a smile, as chances to grow. But more troubling to me was how difficult it became to balance my new responsibilities with my obligations to Team USA. I was waking up every morning at 5 A.M., hustling down to the Harvard gym, working out for two hours, showering, and heading to the office. I worked eight to five, then drove to the rink to skate for a couple of hours. My social life crumbled. I became moody and irritable from exhaustion. My friends and parents clearly noticed that the stress was turning me into another person—I was no longer the Angela they knew. I was losing muscle tone and definition in spite of my efforts to work out. I soon began to feel that I was not able to stay late for work on the days that I wanted to.

I was used to putting my entire being into each task in life, and suddenly I was not able to give everything to the two main things that I wanted. However hard I tried, I could not pursue both a professional business career and a hockey career with any degree of excellence. My balance was off and everything in my life was suffering. I could not use my strategy of focusing clearly on each individual task at hand, because there was simply too much to do. When I was at hockey, I wanted to be at hockey, but often could not stop thinking about the work I was missing. And when I was at work, I worried that I was gradually falling out of shape, while my other teammates were growing and improving. While sitting at my desk, I still dreamt about training and playing hockey for the Women's National Team. And while I was driving to a practice an hour away, I wished I was able to stay late and help Kristin or Tom land another deal.

At the start of 2005, I had to miss a week of work to attend a training camp with Team USA. My bosses were completely understanding about it, but I knew that I couldn't establish the best working relationships with clients if I had to take periodic leaves of absence. Worse, when I arrived at training camp, we tested our physical strength and speed in the weight room and on the ice. My scores were worse than they had ever been. I was out of shape and not training like an elite athlete. Afterward, in my room, I broke down and cried. I decided then and there that I had to make a change.

It won't surprise you to know that I chose hockey over commercial real estate, and it might be fair of you to ask, "What about facing real life? What about being able to make a transition when hockey will no longer be an option?" In many ways, you might think that hockey was my fallback, my safest option, since I knew I was good at it and had done it my whole life. But it wasn't. Staying at Meredith & Grew offered me job security and a place to work when hockey was gone from my life. I was succeeding there, even showing an aptitude for dealing with people and brokering deals. By comparison, hockey offered uncertainty, given the limited options for women to play professionally.

But women's hockey also seemed to be at an important tipping point. Interest in the sport had grown with each Olympics starting in 1998. Team USA played in stadiums packed with more than 10,000 people leading up to the 2002 Games, and the sport has grown in prominence since. The NCAA tournament has increased in competitive quality and attendance each year, girls' hockey registrations continue to climb on the amateur level, and the quality of international play continues to improve. And increasingly, it seems that corporate sponsors and organizers are looking toward a professional league that would combine play in the United States and Canada.

As I wrestled with my decision, I felt an obligation to the game I have played and loved for so long, and I felt an obligation to my Team USA companions and to the young girls coming up through the amateur ranks who currently have nowhere to go beyond college. Performing to the best of my ability was what I needed to do, both to push my team back to the top and to create balance and happiness personally.

Still, it felt like an enormous risk, something I couldn't take lightly. The failure to change is what usually prevents greatness. The limits to our potential are largely imagined. It is hard to venture out into the unknown, for fear of failure or defeat. Most of us think about great things all of the time, but it is the inability to act that prevents us from reaching our true potential. Failing to do all I could to push along the sport and leave a legacy for others to follow would let down those who had gone before me, and those who would come after me. I think if you look at some of the greatest people in the world, they are usually the risk-takers. They see that although there is terror in the unknown, an opportunity is there for the taking. And the degree of risk often multiplies after you realize that you can walk out on a limb and succeed. As someone once said: "Why not go out on a limb? Isn't that where the fruit is?"

▼▼▼

I guess you can say that I have gone out on a few limbs and in the process I have developed confidence in myself. I have fallen a few times along the way, but this has enabled me to learn from my mistakes. A seemingly silly but painful story for me illustrates. When I was in the fifth grade, I wanted to be our school's vice president. I was not the coolest kid in school, but I was also not one of the nerds. I could always talk to both groups of kids, maybe because I was the middle child of our family and had both a brother and a sister. Whatever my position was on the social ladder, I thought that I might have a decent chance at winning in the school's political election.

I rounded up a few of my friends who were willing to cooperate with my political campaign. I decided that I would use the talent of the school's keyboard player and my average acoustics to "rap" my speech to fellow classmates. My friends Heidi and Jason agreed to be my backup "rappers." Because I was short another voice I desperately needed to pull off this campaign stunt, I forced my brother Billy into the group. When election time came, I was nervous but I finally conjured up enough courage to step in front of my entire school to rap my speech. I cannot remember all of the lyrics, but I do recall the first few lines:

"My name is Angela and I am here to say,
I am running for Vice-President today.
I am really loyal to our school,
I have an A-B average and I am really cool."

Then Heidi, Jason, and Billy chimed in with:

"Angela is the best and she won't rest,
until our school is really cool!"

You get the picture. Needless to say, I didn't win. I took a different approach the next time I ran for office, when I was 15 and trying to become the freshman class president at Choate. I spoke from the heart that time and ended up winning the election. I also won the next two offices that I ran for in the tenth and eleventh grades. I was just as nervous, especially remembering the embarrassing rapping incident that I had had years before, but I mustered enough courage to put myself out there, in front of my classmates once again, to judge and to scrutinize me.

Ultimately, this idea of doing something from the heart was the final piece of the puzzle in my decision between job security and hockey. Had I chosen real estate, I don't know that I could have given my heart to it, and that would have been painfully obvious to all I worked for. My heart bled hockey, and I needed to be there.

My hope was to help Team USA succeed at the 2005 World Championships and the 2006 Winter Olympics, then do whatever I could to help launch the sport professionally in the United States or Canada. These were uncharted territories, and it unnerved me, but I knew I needed to focus there and nowhere else. My goals had been set.

▼▼▼

I spoke with my bosses the following week at work. They were very understanding and left the door open for me to come back if my pursuits didn't work out the way I hoped. And then, strangely, things began to work in a way that I couldn't have foreseen. First, I succeeded in getting cleared to play for the Montreal Axion in the Canadian NWHL. Ironically, I ended up playing alongside Team Canada goalie Charline Labonté, who was the first woman to be drafted and play in (men's) junior hockey, in the QMJHL in Canada. I found out later that she played against my brother in the QMJHL, in his very first day in the league. The hockey world is small. I also didn't expect at the time to soon be following Charline's trailblazing ways, in an American men's hockey league.

I loved my time in Montreal, where we spent the season battling teams such as the Brampton Thunder and the Toronto Aeros, making it all the way to the NWHL final game. The ESPN of Canada, TSN, picked up the TV rights to broadcast the championship game. The Stanley Cup, the trophy awarded to the NHL championship team, was on hand that day, sitting in the golden light next to the women's trophy. There was a rumor that the Stanley Cup was going to be presented to the NWHL champion this year, instead of the NHL champion (the financial impasse between players and owners eventually led to the cancellation of the 2004–2005 NHL season), but nothing came of it.

How did I know all of these things? Well, pick up almost any Canadian paper and it will be filled with headline after headline on hockey . . . both women's and men's. I get fired up every time I see one of the Team Canada T-shirts that says, "Canada is Hockey, Hockey is Canada," but it is true. Everyone has played at some point in their lives, in his or her backyard or in the local program. Hell, their $5 bill even depicts a pond hockey scene, complete with a little girl wearing #9 (my old number!), a ponytail sticking out of the back of her helmet, skating with the other hockey-loving kids. Sometimes I feel like I am more well-known in Canada than in the United States, because Canadians love their hockey and respect the game across the lines of nationality. Most of America may not be ready for that kind of devotion, but already in many northern and eastern towns, legions of boys and girls are devoted to hockey and local teams are receiving broader press coverage.

The Axion played in the championship game against the Toronto Aeros. I won the opening face-off on a great play my coach put together, and my pass led to our first goal within five seconds of the clock starting. We scored three more times before becoming too protective of our lead and getting too defensive. We subsequently gave up four unanswered goals.

We lost 5–4, and again it was a painful experience to have worked like we did only to come up short.

▼▼▼

Even so, I took more out of the experience than a loss could take from me. First, the quality of play was as good as it gets in the world—many of the league's players skate for Team Canada or Team USA, and the others who don't are seasoned and talented. Playing with them elevated my game such that I quickly overcame the physical losses I had experienced while working. Second, I saw firsthand how a professional league could take shape and grow. More than 5,000 people attended that final game and countless more watched it live on TV. Sportswriters said that it was one of the best displays of hockey in the world and that it set a high bar for the league in the coming years. To me, it showed clearly that there already exists a sustainable market for the women's game and that the sport is likely to grow.

Playing for the Axion also instilled in me the additional confidence that comes from experience, and this confidence made a huge difference as I rejoined Team USA to prepare for and play in the 2005 World Championships. A winning team has confidence for a reason—its won-loss record. Just ask the Canadian women's hockey team, which exudes confidence at any international event it competes in. The U.S. Women's National Team failed to beat Team Canada in all eight World Championships played from 1990 to 2004, for many reasons, confidence being one of them. While we may have been better than them in a few of those years, we did not finish when it counted.

But 2005 was different. We knew we were setting the stage for the 2006 Olympics. My own sharp improvement while playing for the Axion had helped me grow, and we found in the weeks and days before the tournament a deep connection that helped us believe in each other. As in years past, Canada and the United States rolled through the tournament to the final game. We had the 2002 Olympic loss on our minds, as well as years of frustration from never winning the World Championships.

The game's intensity was relentless, and in most statistical aspects, we dominated throughout . . . except on the scoreboard. While we outshot Canada 49–26 (this was after regulation and overtime) and hit a couple of posts, the score at the end of regulation was 0–0—a testament to the outstanding goaltending on both teams.

We each had one power play in overtime. Canada failed to score, and in our opportunity, we thought we had scored on a shot that pushed goalie Kim St-Pierre back into the net, but no goal was awarded on review.

After the one overtime period, we commenced a "shootout," a rule that the International Ice Hockey Federation uses to determine a winner, rather than unlimited overtime periods. With the ice cleared of players, a single puck carrier charges the net and tries to put a shot past the goalie. Whichever team has scored the most goals after five shots each, wins. This was the first time such a shootout was ever used to secure the winner in the gold medal game.

In the first round, Natalie Darwitz for us and Sarah Vaillancourt (a Harvard freshman) for Canada scored on the same exact shot: top shelf (high in the net), to the goalie's glove side. In the next round, I drew Kim St-Pierre from the goal and slipped in a backhand shot above her pads, putting us up 2–1. I was so in the moment that I forgot how to celebrate, instead opting for the Ray Bourque one-knee-forward-fist-pump. In the third round, neither team scored, but in the fourth round, Krissy Wendell scored another goal on her patented backhand move. And when Chanda Gunn stopped Caroline Ouellette's fourth-round attempt, the game was over, since a fifth round wouldn't have changed the outcome. We were world champions for the first time in history! It was the proverbial dog pile on the winning goaltender, as 20 players mobbed Chanda Gunn. We threw our sticks and gloves into the air and celebrated for nearly ten minutes straight, before they started to hand out the medals. I had watched Canada do this in the last five World Championships. Now, it was our turn.

I was named to the All-Tournament team and given the Directorate Award as the top defenseman. Ultimately, my focus on personal improvement, on being ready to do the best possible job I could when called upon, helped make the difference. My team relied on each other throughout, and when Coach Smith called on me in the shootout, I was happy to help deliver what ended up being the game-winning goal. We couldn't have done it though, without Chanda Gunn in net and the spectacular play of our forwards and defense.

That victory revealed a higher truth, as well. We finally beat Canada in 2005 because we believed in each other and ourselves. That is the thing that separates the best in the world: the mental aspects of the game. It is the ability to focus on the process and not the end goal of wining; it is the ability to have confidence and poise while those around you doubt their ability; it is the synergy of having an entire unit focused on the same goal and being willing to sacrifice for the benefit of the group; it is the ability to be self-aware, enabling us to capitalize when the opportunity presents itself. Ultimately, winning is the ability to reach the zone individually and collectively, the ability to dig deep and use your mind to tell you that you are not tired.

I have felt tired many, many times in my career and it would have been easy for me to give up. When Harvard was losing by five goals in the ECAC championship game years back, my mind had already told me that defeat was inevitable. My legs never felt so tired and heavy. But when we were beating the same team the previous year in the final game by the same number of goals, my legs were as light as can be. You feel pain and fatigue when you are down, and energy and adrenaline when you are winning. This is the mind's ability to drastically change the body, and points to why mental training is such an important part of hockey and life for me.

When I stood ready to take my turn during the shootout, I was focused yet relaxed. I was not thinking about "what if I miss?" but rather trying to read and react to the situation at that moment. Years of experience and mental preparation helped me and my team reach just a bit further, beyond the exhaustion we felt at that time, to outwit the goalie on our shots, and help me put in the winning goal. The ending could have been different—I could have missed or Kim St-Pierre could have made one of her spectacular stops. We could have lost if Chanda had not played flawlessly, or if Krissy and Natalie had failed to put one in during the shootout as well. My stick could have broken, someone could have pulled a muscle, or the other team could have put all five of their shots in the net. The point is that our team did what we could when we were in control of our game, and sat and watched as the rest of the shootout unfolded. This time though, we won.

▾▾▾

Deciding to focus on hockey has worked out for me in a number of ways. The stress of trying to hold it all together had gently strained my family relationships—in the very least, I was not able to put the energy and focus into them that they truly merited. Returning to my training and having more time to see my family changed that measurably. Time itself had also begun to heal and reshape each of my family members.

When I talk with my mother or father now, each is more content with life. They are doing what they love and have come to terms with the divorce and its subsequent pain. Today, I can say comfortably that I am truly happy for where my father is and what he's doing. He has finally learned to follow his passion, and this has made him a happier person. He now has a great job managing a local glass shop, and he has turned into a man that I love and can respect. I also wish I could spend more time with him.

I was always "daddy's little girl" growing up. We used to have conversations that lasted deep into the night. When I left for school my freshman year, we began to drift, as his role in my life gradually diminished. And then in college, I hardly talked to him because of the issues that arose and the subsequent divorce. It wasn't that I didn't love him—I couldn't figure out how best to relate to him, how best to forgive him, nor do I believe he knew how best to relate to me. Time and communication have helped mend our relationship and he has already promised me that he will be cheering in the stands in the 2006 Games. I can't wait for him to finally see me at the sport's largest event.

My mother is my hero. Over the past few years, I have come to appreciate her more. She was the glue that kept our family together when my father struggled during my childhood years. She has always put our family first, above and beyond her own needs. I have learned unconditional love from her—a lesson that I hope to carry into a family of my own and into communities where I work. She also tells me that she prays for me daily—and I guess it is working.

Over the years, it has hurt me to see her deal with such a painful divorce. I know she felt pain not just for her own tattered marriage, but for all of us who suffered through it, as well. She is healing now and living for herself in a way that she never has before. She has found good friends, is enjoying great success as a real estate agent, and she has just started dating.

My parents and we kids struggled for many years while witnessing the break-up of our family. But time has helped us put our relationships back together and build a new foundation for the future. I am no longer running away from my family life, but am embracing it and realizing that whatever comes of it, the best I can do is give all I can to my family and love each member individually. I am even spending this summer training for the 2006 games with Billy and his hockey friends, and spending some quality time at home with Mom and Pam. I know that my family will always be my biggest fans, long after my slapshot stops scoring goals and I no longer play with the USA emblem on my chest.

CHAPTER 8

A Game with the Guys

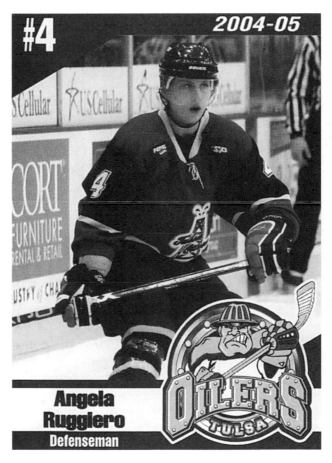

This is my hockey card from my stay with the Tulsa Oilers of the Central Hockey League.

I'm with some young girls at a camp in Michigan where I instruct.

*S*omebody slapped my butt so hard I felt the handprint for a good 30 seconds even after I turned around. This wasn't the kind of assault you expect while walking down the concourse in the Montreal airport, though it's not uncommon when you travel with Team USA, as I was doing. When I turned around, it was Billy. I had not seen him in almost a year and there we were—both in Canada to play a game for our respective teams, me with Team USA and Billy for a QMJHL All-Star squad. This was the first time we crossed paths in such a way. That night was also the first time in our personal history that both of us could be seen playing on a national Canadian television broadcast. I have to say that that was one of the proudest moments for my parents, watching both their children on TV on the same night.

Ever since Billy and I had begun pursuing hockey careers, our opportunities to spend time together had been limited. We're hardly ever in the same time zone, but luckily we're on each other's auto-speed-dial when we need a fix of one another. Hockey, of course, is always the glue that makes us stick. During a conversation after our airport meeting, Billy and I agreed on certain things about my hockey career to date: that it's easier for a woman to succeed in hockey because she can rise through the (numerically limited) ranks more quickly; that we are each other's biggest fans; and that I can still score on him once in a while. We also agreed that in spite of the gender differences in hockey, a good skilled player is a good skilled player.

This last notion must have really stuck with Billy because about a year later, when he was playing for the Tulsa Oilers of the Central Hockey League, it sparked in him an entertaining idea. During one of our frequent telephone conversations in which we regale each other with our recent career highlights, he mentioned to me that he had been joking with his teammates that the team was short on defense and that "my sister should play with us." At that point we hadn't played together for nearly ten years. With both of us now in our mid-twenties, I never expected to get back our youthful days of a brother and sister hockey duo playing on the ice in the same game. But I was wrong. Billy was plotting.

For Billy, what started out as a playful brainstorm soon took on the realm of possibility. He spurred my confidence by telling me that I really was better than his team's defensemen. He said that coming to play with his team in Oklahoma was a unique opportunity, one that would make me the first female hockey player who wasn't a goalie to play professional hockey with men in North America. (Goalie Erin Whitten played in the East Coast Hockey League as well as the Central Hockey League in the early 1990s.) The idea planted a seed and brought me back to our time together on the California Selects when I was 14 years old—the time that my father insisted I be given the opportunity to play, or the team would lose Billy. It wasn't exactly the same situation, but I decided to remain open to the possibility.

After Billy's prodding and pushing the idea onto his coach, the team's management, and the league, I received an invitation to come "skate with the boys" over Christmas 2004. Christmas had looked to be untraditional that year—Mom and Pam had to work over the holidays, and Dad was moved away and onto his new life. As a "Christmas orphan" I fled to the comfort of a home I knew—the ice—and Billy would occupy it, too. Only this time, the ice would be swarming with a bunch of grown, skilled male players in a league renowned not only for the play-ers' size and speed, but also for fights. I knew that I had to keep my head up, but in the end, I wanted to be treated just like one of the guys. No special treatment. No excuses. And no don't-hit-the-girl kind of hockey. I did not want this to be an exercise in chivalry. I wanted to be checked and shoved just like the rest of the boys. While I was bigger than most in the women's game, I knew that my comfort zone was going to be tested in the men's game. This was my opportunity to break into a new level, albeit for a brief moment.

So I flew to Tulsa and, two days before Christmas, suited up for practice. I hit the ice and my heart seemed to rattle around inside my chest. Having Billy by my side and talking me up to the team helped make the experience a little less nerve-racking (only a little, though). I didn't find my rhythmic flow on the ice until the end of practice, which reminded me of my first time on the ice. Just when I started to get into the groove, it was over for the day. As I exited the ice I thought the transition to my desired "zone" would have to pick up exponentially before I entered a game with these guys. A chick wasn't going to have time to be slightly off—that wouldn't fly. When you're called to play, just like a guy being called up for the first time, you better be on. No excuses. The 2002 Olympic game flashed in my head—what if everything seemed to go wrong? I kept repeating two mantras over and over to myself: What you can't control has to leave your head. Focus on what you know and control that.

As it turned out I got called back to the Montreal Axion training camp shortly after that first practice with the Oilers, and had to postpone plans to play in a men's game. In mid-January, however, I signed a one-day contract with the Oilers and the team issued a press release. I would play in a Friday-night game on January 28 in Tulsa, against the Rio Grande Killer Bees, setting history as the first female skater to play in a CHL game as well as being part of the first-ever brother-sister duo in a professional game. A portion of the game's proceeds were to go to the Tsunami Relief Fund of the Red Cross, and girls 12 and under were being let in for free. A sell-out crowd of close to 6,000 was expected.

▼▼▼

I flew in on a Wednesday to get a few practices in before the game. Billy picked me up at the Tulsa airport. Days before I had chopped my blonde hair to a chin-length bob, the shortest I had ever worn my hair. Billy took one look at me and said, "Did you get a haircut?"

"Yes."

"Man, the guys are going to give me a bad time. My hair is longer than yours now."

Billy had the quintessential "hockey hair"—just long enough and shaggy enough to stick out from under the helmet. Once on the ice among the boys, my hair would be a non-issue, since you wouldn't even be able to see it when I put on a helmet. No long blond braids marking an "X" on my back this time. With our near-identical haircuts, clear aquamarine eyes, and squared jaws, Billy and I almost looked like fraternal twins.

We traveled to a press conference with about twenty different media personnel waiting to fire questions at me. When I entered the room I first met with the team owner, general manager, and public relations director. I saw the head coach, Butch Kaebel, and I immediately asked him about playing time. I did not want this to become a sideshow, a publicity stunt, a farce. I wanted it to be a legitimate and meaningful experience that raised money for the Red Cross, inspired young girls, and that gave me professional hockey experience. I wanted more than a single token shift on the ice. He assured me that I'd get a regular shift in the first period. I asked if I could play more. He said he'd see what he could do.

When I approached the podium with its spread of microphones, displayed like an intricate Oriental silk fan, I felt completely unprepared. It was the same set-up you'd see when a star player signs with a new NHL team. Behind me the team's icon—a burley, clinched-jaw player with a high stick—blazed on fabric. Butch introduced me and handed me the specially made team jersey: Ruggiero, No. 4. Not only my name but my number made me smile. I proceeded to put it on and didn't stop smiling. I led off with a few opening remarks about my gratitude for the opportunity to play with the Oilers, to play with my brother, and for the great cause. After I unleashed the phrase to the crowd, "So do you have any questions?" a whirlwind of reporters' hands shot up.

"How did you conceive the idea?"

"Are you afraid to get hit?"

"Do you think Billy will come out of the net if some guy runs you?"

"Is this a publicity stunt?"

"Are you nervous?"

"How does this compare to the Olympics?"

"Where will you shower and change?"

"What is the difference between men's and women's hockey?"

"Tell us about the humanitarian component to this."

"Do you think women will ever play in the NHL?"

"Do you see yourself as a trailblazer for girls and women?"

"What impact will this have on women in sports and women in general?"

"How much do you expect to play?"

"Who were your idols growing up?"

"How will it feel to play alongside your brother for the first time in 10 years?"

"How close are the two of you?"

"Is this a proud moment for your family?"

"What words of advice would you send to girls and women?"

"Would you consider playing professionally in the future?"

In two words, the press conference was exhilarating and exhausting. The attention continued unabated when it was over. My phone did not stop ringing the entire time I was there. Whenever I answered it, a producer or reporter from a national media outlet wanted an interview—"The Today Show," ESPN's "Cold Pizza," *The Hockey News, Detroit Free Press, Detroit News, Ventura County Star, The Globe and Mail, Toronto Star, ESPN The Magazine,* Vancouver radio stations, *Boston Globe,* and so on. The personalized attention surprised me. Hockey had always been a team sport, which was one of the factors (in addition to my hockey-crazed father) that drew me to it in the first place. I'd always found that sharing the dynamics of leadership, creating a structure among individuals on the ice, and working towards the same goal were less daunting and more rewarding than what a solo sport offered. The focus on me as an individual made me uncomfortable, but I decided that this was a personal "comfort-zone" issue I was going to have to conquer. I just hoped I'd get over it and calm my nerves before starting the game. I recalled the Olympics, when I knew that many eyes were on me but I tried to ignore them just the same.

No pressure not to fall and make a fool of yourself, Angela. In the back of my mind I caught a glimmer of one of my first practices with the Women's National Team, when I had fallen down and missed shots and played so raggedly that my eyes had welled with tears. Then I reminded myself: I was 15 then. Now, I was 25. Life had changed. My biggest concern was calming myself and just playing hockey, the kind that had catapulted me this far. I could do that.

In my mind, I visualized the perfect game. Fast shots. Agility on the blades. Simple but tough defense. I don't generally remember my dreams on the night before a big game, and on that particular night, nothing was different until nerves woke me up the next morning. I felt the pressure on my shoulders as an individual player for this game. The players, coaches, media, everyone would be watching to see how I handled myself in a league of men.

When I got to the rink for a two-hour morning skate, the team's equipment manager helped me out and put a half-shield on my helmet. I wanted to fit in with the rest of the guys. No longer behind the full protective glass or cage of the amateur, collegiate, and international world, I decided to put my lower face, including my jaw and teeth, out there for possible whacking. As I placed the helmet over my head and felt it snug against my forehead, I looked out and realized how clear the world was. And, in that instant, I was doing exactly what I wanted to do. Commuting to a desk job and clicking a mouse all day were elements of a life I had taken on that didn't mesh with the dream that I had held onto since a young girl: to be a professional hockey player. Working a full-time job while trying to squeeze in an individualized and intense training schedule each day for the Olympics was not cutting it. Wherever I was, I wasn't *there*.

I finally understood the double-edged sword of freedom versus time. Money allows a certain amount of freedom but cuts into the freedom of time. And I realized I didn't need much money for happiness. I believe when you follow your passion, life is easier to deal with. When you're going against what it is you're supposed to be doing, life becomes unbalanced very quickly. You have to decide what it is you can live without to pursue a passion. For me it has been about keeping very little to my name. I live a rather bohemian life—my only asset is a new car, a cute red Jetta. I can fit everything I need in life within that car as I travel to and from various training camps across the continent. I don't see this lifestyle ending anytime soon, though one day I want to get married, have kids, and settle into a house. Then again, that's a future beyond my control at this moment because the opportunities have not presented themselves. Until I round the next corner of my life, I am living in this moment of a dream fulfilled as a woman playing professional hockey.

My dream had currently placed me here in Oklahoma, perhaps an unlikely site to make hockey history. This proves you never know when a wild idea anywhere in the world can become something significant. I changed my underclothes in my own locker room, twenty feet or so from the team's locker room. Then I went into the men's locker room to put on my gear. I felt quieter than usual. I wasn't dancing to the music in my iPod. I was in my gear but I wasn't in my skin.

When we hit the ice we started practicing drills that were identical to the ones I had done at Harvard and with the

Women's National Team. Hockey was hockey. The root of it was the same no matter what league you played in. The men moved the puck with such fierceness and speed that I couldn't help but smile. My specialty in the women's game translated to the men's arena as well, since I loved looking up the ice with the puck, finding a perfect seam between defenders and going tape-to-tape with a crisp pass to a streaking Krissy Wendell or Katie King or Natalie Darwitz. The men make every single pass hard and accurate. I thought, *If I constantly played at this level, my game would improve dramatically.*

Reporters and cameramen were on the sidelines for most of the practice. Jaroslav Cesky, an outstanding forward from Prague, joked with me, "Hey, want to pass with me, so that I can get on the camera, too?" The men started warming up to me by mid-practice. I was reminded of my youth days when the boys on the team were my best friends. They respected me and really didn't look at me differently. But this was the pros and it takes several years for any player—let alone a woman—to garner the respect of the league's players. I knew I was not just one of the boys and that everyone would be watching me as a representative of the women's game. I didn't know whether the men would tend to go really hard to prove a point, or back off altogether because they didn't know how to act or play with a woman. I was prepared for any slander on the ice and for the skeptics that came there to watch me fail.

The next day the lightheartedness of the team continued. They placed a dancing Canadian beaver with a hockey stick in my stall, mocking my U.S. citizenship since three-fourths of the team were Canadian. I also found that one of the guys had placed a "C" for captain on my jersey and requested that I lead the stretch, since I had been getting all the attention. Giving me a hard time was the icing on the cake to fitting in with this clan of scruffy faces. This was what I wanted from the group—no special girl treatment.

The morning before the game, Billy picked me up for an interview on ESPN's "Cold Pizza." He wore his Oilers track suit and I wore my USA Hockey jacket. Bill Clement interviewed us for about three minutes. The Oilers' owners and coaches never expected this kind of national media frenzy. It ended up being a big boost for the team's ticket and merchandise sales.

The interview and the media circus around the rink made us a little late for the pregame ritual. The team jokingly fined me ten dollars for tardiness. After a 40-minute warmup skate, we rushed to do a radio interview. The next interview, for "The Today Show," required a little more personal prep time, with a quick shower, makeup application, and hair styling. Billy and I recalled childhood memories of what it was like to grow up as hockey players and best friends who spent practically every spare minute together in the car or on the ice.

After two more interviews that day I finally hibernated in my hotel room, took another shower for the pure relaxation of it, and brewed myself some coffee in the room. I didn't even turn on the television or radio. I just sat quietly on the bed in my towel and drank the hot coffee. It felt so peaceful to sit alone and to casually lie on the bed for two hours drifting in and out of a nap.

A few hours before game time, Billy picked me up in his Ford pickup. He had Mom with him in the front and she squeezed into the middle, periodically glancing side to side at her hockey kids. (This game was to be another without Dad, as he was living in Washington State and could not get off of work.) Mom had flown in the night before and wasn't going to miss this night of history. We knew she probably wanted to take advantage of the moment by talking about the wild trajectories of our lives, but we told her that both of us liked to be quiet before a big game. Instead we focused on the music and sat in silence. Though we didn't talk, it didn't matter. I could feel her love when I looked over to see her smiling and looking at the road ahead.

This particular game night was unlike any other I'd known. Hours before the game, I usually sit and think about the various situations that might occur on the ice. I study the dimensions of the rink and check to see how much space is behind the net, because every rink differs. I usually tape my stick while gazing onto the ice surface and visualizing the game that has not yet been played. Not this time. More pregame interviews were scheduled. I couldn't help but think what great preparation the Olympics had been for this nonstop press junket. You had to simultaneously focus on the questions while not losing complete focus on the task at hand: playing hockey.

Instead of my usual routine, I instead jumped on the exercise bike for ten minutes and then stretched. I was in the locker room with the men, and "The Today Show" followed me around, again. Nike had sent me five sticks that the organization wanted me to tape and use for a silent auction and donation to the Hockey Hall of Fame. The camera came in close as I wrapped a stick; the camera panned out to a full body shot as I wrapped a stick.

Geared up, I finally hit the ice a little before game time to shake the jelly from my legs. I reminded myself of an effective playing philosophy: *Keep it simple.* My goal, as it was in the first Olympics, was to play stay-at-home defense, rather than the more freewheeling, offensive-minded, Bobby Orr style of defense I'd become used to playing. I didn't want the men to beat me out there, so I decided to take few chances and minimize risk.

Back in the locker room minutes before we took the ice for game time, the coach went over again the systems and the D-zone, which were pretty close to what I was used to playing in Montreal. I was second in line as the team filed to exit onto the ice. The lights in the rink were dim and the guy behind me whispered, "Be careful not to trip on the carpet. It happens all the time." From behind the half-shield I turned my head and flashed him a smile and wink. I pretty much ignored the stands and the fans, with the exception of immediately finding Mom in her seat. And on my glance to find her I saw someone's sign that read "Title IX Works." Under my skin, layers of chills built and then culminated at the base of my neck. If only for a couple of hours in Tulsa, I knew this game was for women beyond hockey. I was breaking a barrier. I wanted to prove to everyone—just as the young girl in me had—that women could compete with men.

The announcer called out the starting line-ups. Mario Joly, the six-foot-four, 230-pound defenseman I would be playing with, then the three forwards, Billy, and then me. My adrenaline pumped so fast I forgot to stand next to Billy on the blue line during the introductions. The Killer Bees defensemen were on average older, stronger, and taller. *Keep it simple. Hockey is hockey.*

As we stood listening to the U.S. anthem I felt proud— I hadn't heard it in more than a year because I had been playing in Canada. Hearing it again brought to mind all that I had experienced: the 1998 Olympics, various world championships, carrying the World Trade Center flag in the 2002 Olympics, and the hundreds of times I had heard the anthem at other venues over the years. The anthem carries a lot of weight for me . . . because of what it represents broadly for our nation and what it has meant to me personally throughout the years. I was also very familiar with the Canadian anthem, as Dad had taught me to play both the U.S. and the Canadian anthem on the piano as a kid. We even celebrated, along with the Fourth of July, Canada Day on July 1, not because we were Canadian, but out of the pure joy of loving hockey.

My first shift was one of my best in the entire game. I came out fired up and the puck whisked over to my stick. I passed to the center man for a clean breakout. I moved up the ice and then got off about one minute into the game. Even so, the more I played, the more I felt at home. As in other big games in my life I reiterated my mantra: *Get a couple of shifts out of the way and then settle into the game.* Often, when it comes to big games, I can't seem to remember much of the first period. I do remember the crowd went wild when I threw a hip check on an opposing player in my third shift of the game. They sure do love the physical aspect of the game in Tulsa. The men pushed and I pushed back. Even as a kid, I was never afraid of contact because I felt that my skill and strength worked to my advantage. I ended up playing a regular shift in the first and third periods. I got off of the ice and gave interviews for the entire time between the first and second periods. The rest of the time I sat on the bench and cheered on the rest of the team. It was great to just sit on the bench and see these professional athletes do their thing . . . and to watch Billy from the sidelines. He was playing so well and I was so proud of him.

I finished the game with a "plus-2," meaning that my team scored two more goals than the other team while I was on the ice. (Since defensemen aren't often high scorers, this is a useful statistic to rate their overall effect on a game.) I even managed an assist on the final goal. With 8 seconds remaining in the game, the guys on my team kept telling me to jump into the offensive play, like I usually do. I did so, prevented the puck from leaving the zone, and whisked a backhand pass to one of my teammates, who scored the final goal in our 7–2 victory. Funny thing was that the guys all came to congratulate me for my assist rather than the player who scored the goal. I was later selected as the "first star" for the game and even got a trading card in the team's set for the year.

After the game, officials from the Hockey Hall of Fame, which is in Toronto, collected jerseys and sticks from me and Billy, to immortalize the Ruggieros in the museum. Now this wasn't something Billy and I had discussed while Dad drove us to practice in Pasadena all those years ago.

▼▼▼

My one game with the Tulsa Oilers was historic but other women have blazed a similar path. Perhaps the most prominent trailblazer is Canadian player Hayley Wickenheiser, the all-time leading scorer for the Canadian National Team and one of the best female hockey players in the game today. She left North America to play for a Finnish men's professional hockey league. She could have played for a women's professional league in

Europe, but chose the more physical and competitive play in the men's league.

I also need to mention Cammi Granato, a fixture on the U.S. Women's National Team. She's the most recognizable face of the game today, and the all-time leading scorer in the women's game. She has been a great pioneer to the sport and she has helped the game move into the next millennium, much like what Mia Hamm has been able to do for women's soccer. Not only is Cammi an amazing player and an effective ambassador, but she is also an inspiring leader. I have learned a ton about the game from her. I always look to her in the locker room for inspiration because she has been there from the beginning and knows how to play the game. If you ever have the chance to learn from a great person, do it. For me, Cammi has been fundamental in my growth as a player and person.

People sometimes ask me if I think hockey will ever be fully integrated between the genders, if we'll have men and women routinely playing against each other. I compare the situation to the trajectory distance runners have taken. Women weren't allowed to run in most marathons until the 1970s, and it wasn't until 1973 that the first all-women's marathon was held, in Waldniel, West Germany. As late as the 1980 Summer Olympics held in Moscow, Olympic distance races for women were limited to the 1,500-meter race (less than a mile). Since then, women's distance running has grown enormously, there's an Olympic marathon for women, and the spread between women's record times and men's record times has gradually shrunk. For example, Margaret Okayo's 2:20:43 winning time for women at the 2002 Boston Marathon would have been good enough to win the entire race as recently as 1968 (when the unofficial time, because women were not allowed entry, for the winning woman was 3:30:00). In ultra-distance races (100 miles, or more, often run over several days), in fact, women have begun to place first overall. Physiologists say that women's greater fat stores, and perhaps a greater ability to bear pain (think childbirth, men), may give women the advantage in such races.

Running is a noncontact sport, and with the exception of the ultra-long distances men have a physical advantage that is likely to keep them ahead of the women. Women aren't generally as interested in competing directly against men as they are in having their female side of the sport put on equal footing with that of the men. Similarly, in hockey, I don't think women want to play in the men's NHL—the physical differences between men and women are too great. Consider that the average NHL player is six-foot-one, 200 pounds, while the average women's hockey player is around five-foot-seven, 154 pounds.

Most women hockey players don't feel a burning desire to mix it up with the men, nor to subject themselves to the nightly pounding men undergo—particularly with such a size discrepancy. Like women runners, we do want our sport on an even footing with that of the men, and we're working to that end. Now that women's hockey is on the map, women are doing the same kinds of strength and conditioning training that men have done. The game is elevating, and individual players are pushing the limits. Take a few minutes and watch Tricia Dunn, Jamie Hagerman, or Kathleen Kauth of the USA team train and you will see what I mean. These players, along with the rest of the team, push their physical limits every day in order to pursue our shared dream of another Olympic gold. Personally, I'm not begging to play in a men's league. I would if it would help me become a better hockey player, and have even considered playing with the men over in Europe after the next Olympics, but if there is a women's league that can help me excel, I'll take that instead.

But that feeling doesn't diminish the importance of the occasional barrier-breaking event. Women crossing over for occasional appearances in men's venues creates tremendous exposure that we hope increases the audience for the women's game. Even if people don't have, say, video clips of my game with Billy, many more people have heard about it. What I would like people to realize is that I held my own in that game, and that you can see similar play from me and other women on our national teams and in our growing professional leagues. Strengthening the sport in this way is where my heart is going.

▼▼▼

Following your heart is never an exact science. And you never know where you're going to end up when you do. The Tulsa game placed my life into perspective: I wanted to do what I loved and that was hockey. Working in the corporate world with a steady schedule didn't allow the freedom of choice that I had so revered in my life. My youthful life of travel and adventure had not prepared me for the monotony I experienced when sitting still. Before I went to Tulsa, Mom spoke to me about choices. She said that I still had choices in my young life. She could hear the unhappiness in my voice while working full-time and trying to train full-time.

Part of me knows I'm just beginning my inroads into hockey. I still have my eyes set on both the 2006 and the 2010

Olympics. People often ask me, what then? Well, I'll just have turned 30 before hitting the ice in the 2010 Olympics, which is a great decade to start another phase in my young life. Wherever I am or whatever I do, I'll always continue with the no-regrets approach to my life. Those who say that you have to stick to a traditional path in life never took a chance on dreams. Those are not the people who set records—in history or in their personal lives. Don't misplace your life because you've lost something, but learn from what you lose. You could shave years off your life trying to find the answers to what it is you really want, but in that time, don't forget to dream immediately and fulfill those short-term goals.

As I step into a five-year plan for my life, I see many options. I might return to business school and earn my MBA. I might become a collegiate hockey coach. I might join a men's or women's European hockey league. I might open up a hockey school. I might find my soulmate and get married. I might even rejoin Meredith & Grew, or perhaps just head back to Michigan for a while and catch up with Mom and play with our Great Danes.

When I go back to Michigan, I pass through Harrison Township, which has a welcome sign that reads: "Home to Angela Ruggiero, 1998 Gold Medalist." Though my family lived there only for a short time, the town still claims me. When I see it, it always makes me chuckle a little at the thought of a place wanting to claim me, hold me down to a home, when I can barely claim one permanent address anywhere or anytime in my life. Home has never been a specific place, but wherever Mom resides. As I cross the world on adventures, I always place her address as my "home" on applications and forms. If she moves anywhere else, I'll continue to follow her as do my personal artifacts.

Boxes of hockey memorabilia, trophies, and other accolades filled one half of my bedroom in Michigan. As a kid, Dad had a hockey shrine of our accomplishments in the living room. Now, in the den, there are a few newspaper clippings and trophies of our hockey careers. When I was younger, I strove to earn individual medals and awards. The older I get, the more personal accolades mean less, and team accomplishments mean much more. In the end, you are only as good as those who stand beside you, in life and on the ice.

I guess I have to agree with Thomas Jefferson's famous saying that, "I find the harder I work, the more luck I seem to have." I have been blessed my entire life and somehow things have always worked out for me. I am not sure if there is any exact science to life and hockey, but I try to live for the day and plan for tomorrow. Hockey has given me so much in my first 25 years of life and I will hopefully play into my sunset years. For now, I will sit back and enjoy each moment I get to spend with my teammates, for they have been the ones that have made this ride worthwhile. I can guarantee you that there is no better feeling as an athlete than to win a gold medal at the Olympics with the group of women you can call your friends. And this is all I can ask for.

Epilogue

David Silverman

I'm keeping my eye on the puck here during a game against St. Lawrence University at the 2004 NCAA championship tournament.

David Silverman

The Harvard Women's Team lines up during the 2004 NCAA championship tournament.

The growth of women's hockey in the United States has been accelerating rapidly in the last 15 years. Although the first recorded women's hockey game was played in 1891, the sport itself has had a relatively quiet history until my lifetime. In the 1920s, colleges began to have women's teams, but many of those died off in the 1940s and 1950s as women replaced men in the economy and then, with the return of the soldiers, focused on raising families. Additionally, the popularity of the men's game grew rapidly during that time, which meant that women's ice time across the country was much more limited.

Finally, in the 1970s, U.S. colleges resurrected women's hockey programs, and varsity and club teams, especially in the Midwest and the Northeast, began popping up. Girls began joining youth hockey leagues in small but growing numbers. The first Amateur Hockey Association national championship for girls and women happened in the early 1980s, and in 1984 Providence College won the first Eastern College Athletic Conference Women's Championship. A Women's World Invitational Tournament was held in North York and Mississauga, Ontario, in 1987. Its success, combined with that of the European Women's Championship in 1989, spurred the International Ice Hockey Federation to hold the first Women's World Championship in 1990. Recognition as an Olympic sport followed in 1998, and in 1999–2000, the first quasi-professional league in North America, the National Women's Hockey League of Canada, was established.

Women's hockey is now the fastest growing sport in Canada and one of the fastest growing in the United States. It seems natural, then, that the next step of progression will be a full professional league that includes broadcast coverage, national and cross-border interest, players commanding reasonable salaries, and owners building rinks and making money from an established fan base.

The experience of other women's sports in the United States shows that the growth of professional women's hockey has to be managed carefully and wisely, or the sport won't make it. For example, the Women's National Basketball Association (WNBA) has been the most significant professional women's sports league established in the last ten years. In many ways, it enjoys what all female athletes would like to see for their sport—significant sponsorship, broad media coverage, and patience for growth and profit. With David Stern, the (men's) NBA commissioner, backing the idea, the league was announced in 1996 and play began in June 1997. NBC, ESPN, and Lifetime all signed on for broadcast rights, and the WNBA played during the late summer when there is little besides baseball to compete with. In the first season, more than 50 million viewers watched games on the three networks, and in 2001, when ESPN2 also joined in broadcasting games, broadcasts reached 60 million fans who spoke 23 languages in 167 countries.

Sounds fabulous, right? The WNBA actually faces many threats. To date, it has still not turned a profit. Its collective bargaining agreement with players runs out in 2007—the first year that the league believes it will earn a profit. That wouldn't necessarily be cause for concern, but women's basketball is well established in Europe, where players can sign with a team in Russia, for example, and make as much as $150,000 . . . just for playing during the playoffs. By comparison, the WNBA minimum salary for a veteran of four years is just $45,427, and the league maximum is $89,000. Even this discrepancy wouldn't be much of a problem, except that the European leagues tend to overlap portions of their schedules with U.S. training camps. Thus, returning U.S. players often miss large portions of camp and ultimately hurt their teams. And with money being an issue, it's virtually guaranteed that the discussion in 2007 for contract renewals will be at least somewhat contentious. Already, one WNBA team has folded, and others are reportedly in financial trouble. Hence, though the league enjoys deep pockets from investors and sponsors, and though it receives excellent media coverage and TV deals, its survival is by no means guaranteed.

Even more instructive is the case of U.S. women's soccer. Few can forget the summer of 1999 and that heart-pounding round of penalty kicks against China, with the United States ultimately prevailing to win the Women's World Cup in front of 60 million viewers. Youth soccer was already exploding across the country, and girls signed up in droves to be like the new heroes they had seen on TV. It seemed a perfect moment to go forward with a professional league. Organizers envisioned something like the WNBA model with robust media rights, large stadium venues, and deep-pocketed corporate sponsors who could afford to be patient for profit and growth. Just three years after its promising launch, the Women's United Soccer Association (WUSA) folded, citing a $20 million revenue shortfall. Just 7,000 people attended the final championship game. Organizers hope to relaunch the league in the near future, but with a different business model and greatly revised expectations.

Admittedly, the WUSA faced some unforeseen challenges. The economic downturn of 2001 limited corporate sponsorship.

Perhaps more crucial, organizers found that the media was reluctant to embrace widespread coverage of the games. ESPN continues to cater to a largely male audience, and its programming of women's sports has only gradually increased in the last few years. In many ways, WUSA organizers most likely overestimated the level of committed viewership and the number of paying spectators necessary to help the sport grow.

▼▼▼

Women's professional softball has had a longer history than women's professional basketball and soccer. In 1976, tennis legend Billie Jean King, former pro golfer Jane Blaylock, and renowned softball player Joan Joyce launched a professional softball league. The league hung around for four seasons but ultimately died from a lack of funding. Then, in 1989, former Utah State softball player Jane Cowles handed her parents a business plan for a professional women's softball league. Her parents happened to own the Cowles Media Company and were thus in a position to back the league. Market research and testing occurred over a six-year period and included numerous exhibition games, a barnstorming tour, and other initiatives. With the corporate sponsorship of AT&T Wireless in 1996–1997, the Cowles organized the league.

The league has teams in both small-market (Akron, Ohio; Lowell, Massachusetts) and large-market (Houston, Chicago) venues. The league has seen its share of ups and downs—it has had three different names, and it suspended play in 2002 in order or pursue a rebranding strategy and possible expansion teams. Nevertheless, professional softball has largely succeeded as a media attraction: ESPN and ESPN2 have broadcast various games, and between 1999 and 2001, the 30 games ESPN2 broadcast consistently outrated both Major League Soccer and the NHL. In 2003, similar to how the NBA supports the WNBA, Major League Baseball (MLB) signed on as a development partner. MLB opened the doors for the National Pro Fastpitch league to work with MLB sponsors, teams, and broadcast partners.

Today, the women's league has six teams that play 48 games in a season. Its main marketing strategy remains at the grassroots level, though the mixture of Major League Baseball and broadcast deals with ESPN and ESPN2 demonstrate the league's desire to get out of small venues and grow the audience base. Prospects seem reasonably good, but the process for women's softball has been long and full of pitfalls.

▼▼▼

Where does women's hockey fit into this picture? For women's hockey to really make it in this already saturated world of sports and entertainment, we desperately need to get it into the print and broadcast media. There are a million options when it comes to sports, and we need to have compelling enough games and stories that we drive interest in audiences and thus interest in the media. I find myself frustrated and disheartened at times when I flip through the channels, only to find a celebrity bowling game on or a championship game of curling. (Sorry, Canadians, I know curling's big up there, but I just don't get its appeal.) Women's hockey has managed to make it onto the sports highlight shows in recent years, but the fact is that the world tunes in to our sport only every four years . . . just like most Olympic sports.

I can still remember playing in the first nationally televised game in 1997 on our pre-Olympic tour. Lifetime, "television for women," had decided to pick up a game against Canada. We disappointed the American sports fans that day, blowing a three-goal lead, but nonetheless, it was an important first step for women's hockey. Just like any sport, fans need a way to connect with and follow their teams on a day-to-day basis. I hope that one day there will be endless streams of media that feed every fan's desire for the game.

When I was 14 I had to select a foreign language as a course requirement. My father recommended selecting French as my foreign language of choice when I entered Choate, arguing that I would be able to use it "when you go to Canada one day to play hockey." I hate to say that he was right, but he was. I used the odd sentence here and there in French-speaking Montreal in 2005, playing for the Montreal Axion of the NWHL. This professional league, consisting of nine teams in the eastern part of Canada, fields some of the best competition in the world. Many of the Canadian players that do not play for the formidable Olympic Oval program in Calgary are part of the NWHL. But the rule that prohibits no more than two non-Canadians on any team has to be lifted if the NWHL wants the best players and increased visibility, keys for the long-term sustainability of the league. To fully succeed, women's hockey and the NWHL should also consider expanding to border locations in the United States, such as Detroit and Buffalo. The league is already off of the ground . . . and like any endeavor, it sorely needs committed sponsors to help reach this goal!

Expectations also have to be closely managed. The most recent championship game in the NWHL drew slightly more than 5,000 fans. This is a robust number for almost any women's hockey game in the world, but it's not a terribly rousing number for a lot of corporate sponsors. After all, a recent Minnesota high school state championship boys' hockey game drew more than 16,000 fans. But that doesn't mean there isn't a viable business model. At least initially, women's hockey has to think less like the WNBA and the WUSA and more like a minor league men's baseball or hockey league. Those leagues build smaller venues, and they help their players become integral parts of the community. They reach into the small towns where large professional leagues won't go. Minor league baseball, for one, is enjoying huge growth in rural America, in part because Americans want live, inexpensive sports entertainment, and only the largest cities have big-league teams.

There is another women's professional league, in Switzerland. The competition is not nearly as fierce as that of the NWHL, but imported players who play in this league are treated like royalty. It is the only league in the world where players are paid in addition to having living expenses such as a car and rent paid for. A few of my American teammates have played over there and have had the opportunity to not only play hockey, but also see the world. Not a bad living if you play games, ski the Alps, and slip in a weekend trip to Milan.

I know that the game will continue to grow in Canada, and hopefully in the United States, with continued support from the media and from aggressive, early-entrant sponsors such as Nike. Nike, for example, has consistently seen women's athletics as high-potential, high-growth markets and has responded by being one of the first significant sponsors to sign players to endorsement deals, provide equipment for teams, and push athletes into the media spotlight. Nike has signed me, Cammi Granato, and Cassie Campbell, among others, to promotional contracts; you see the swoosh all over Team USA apparel at the Olympics and the Women's World Championships; and Nike is working closely with the media to promote women hockey players at the 2006 Olympics and beyond. Developments like these are critical to the game's growth and survival in North America because they bring female hockey players into American living rooms and make them household names and embodiments of the sport for future players to look up to and parents to point out as role models.

But the area that I am most concerned about is overseas. For the sport to flourish in the long run and in the Olympics, teams like Sweden, Finland, China, Germany, and Russia have to catch up to the top two. There are clear echelons in our sport and these have to disappear in order for the fans to tune in to a truly global and competitive sport. I have to add here that if you look at the men's side of the game, Canada and then the Soviet Union clearly dominated for decades before any other nations turned their programs into gold-caliber teams . . . meaning that you have to give our brand time to grow. I just hope that in the process of gaining exposure for our sport here in North America, our competition puts some much needed resources into their women's teams and helps elevate the game to the next level. I am putting a challenge out there . . . and hopefully I retire before a Finland or a Sweden beats the USA, but I would eventually like to see it for the greater good of the game.

▼▼▼